PETER F. [obscured by label]

Ministry and Management

The Study of Ecclesiastical Administration

Foreword by
Professor A. T. Hanson, D.D.

TAVISTOCK PUBLICATIONS
in association with
HICKS SMITH & SONS

First published in 1968
by Tavistock Publications Limited
11 New Fetter Lane, London E C 4
and printed in Great Britain
in 10 pt Plantin
by Butler and Tanner Ltd
Frome and London

1.1
SBN 422 71970 6

First published as a Social Science Paperback in 1968
1.1
SBN 422 72480 7

Distributed in the USA
by Barnes & Noble Inc.

To all who are called
to any office and administration in the church

Contents

PART THREE · THE PRACTICE OF ECCLESIASTICAL ADMINISTRATION

Foreword

It is frequently said today that academic study is suffering from excessive fragmentation. Despite the efforts that have been made, particularly in the newly founded universities, to change this trend, each branch of learning is growing more specialized, and it is becoming increasingly difficult to be really learned in more than one area of any subject. Against this tendency Dr Peter Rudge's book bears admirable witness. He is qualified in both Theology and Sociology, and he has made use of his expertise to explore an area where these two disciplines overlap. We have of course plenty of works which *seem* to cover this area, books on the sociology of religion, and more or less technical books on church administration. Many of them will be found in Dr Rudge's bibliography. But it seems to me that Dr Rudge has done something more than just write a book on the sociology of religion, or on church administration. He has used his sociological insights to illuminate his theological insights. He looks at the church from the point of view of a sociologist, but he also knows, and values, the church from the inside. This gives a special quality to his book and means, I believe, that it has a special claim on the attention of theologians and church leaders as well as of sociologists and experts in management. As far as I am competent to judge, it seems to me that he has neither let his theology prejudice his sociology, nor allowed his sociology to debunk his theology. Each, as I have suggested, illuminates the other.

Writing, however, as one who has no qualifications whatever in Sociology, I think it may be helpful to say something to those who are in a similar case about how one should read this book. I would emphasize that it is very important to read on to the end. It may be confusing at first, since Dr Rudge appears to be making a large number of *a priori* statements about administration, and to be satiating us with theory before showing us its relevance. If you persevere, you will see that his theory is applied in practice, and its relevance for anyone concerned with church administration does become clear at the end. He wants us, if I understand him rightly, to apply to our practice the categories which he provides, to ask ourselves whether we are proceeding on a classical or a charismatic basis, and so on. The answer will almost certainly be complicated, and we shall find, if we are honest, that we are sometimes proceeding on one basis and sometimes on another. As he makes clear, there is nothing to be ashamed of in this: the important thing is to be aware of what we are doing.

From the point of view of a theologian, it seems to me that the main value of this book is that it helps us to keep our feet on the ground. Dr Rudge is not attempting to prove that what we imagine to be theological insights are really mere reactions to social pressures; but he is helping us to understand how our theological insights work out, and is therefore to that extent enabling us to make the insights of Christianity more effective in contemporary society. Such a study as this is most appropriate to a religion which has at its centre a doctrine of incarnation, and which therefore must have an empirical element in it.

I can well imagine that Dr Rudge's book will establish itself as an authoritative study of an area upon which the illumination of sociological research has not previously been directed in any comparable way.

In the universities, not only will theologians and social scientists welcome this book, but also students reading some of the degree courses at honours level that are planned with a view to giving a synoptic view of a number of disciplines: for example, European civilization and the history of Western institutions. Finally, it is much to be hoped that Dr Rudge's book will inspire others to cultivate this field.

ANTHONY HANSON

University of Hull
July 1968

Author's Preface

This book springs out of a somewhat unusual career, the two threads of which have only recently been brought together.

The first, the administrative interest, began with commercial courses at secondary school, developed into a Bachelor of Commerce degree at the University of Tasmania, and reached its climax in the Diploma of Public Administration.

It seemed, then, that all this was left behind when I entered St Michael's House in Adelaide to train for the ministry of the Church of England in Australia, the training being followed by some ten years in parishes of the Diocese of Canberra and Goulburn.

However, experience in the ministry with positions of growing responsibility led to the realization that the earlier administrative training was at least equal in value to the theological training; and there seemed to be a definite possibility that an administrative study might be developed for the guidance of those who held office in the church. Preliminary thoughts were in terms of a simple transposition of public administration into the ecclesiastical realm, and the parallel gave rise to the term 'ecclesiastical administration'.

This is the subject that I set out to develop when I went to England in 1963. At St Augustine's College, Canterbury, I had the opportunity to write a dissertation entitled *A New Approach to the Study of Ecclesiastical Administration*; and I can recall the examiner stating that this was not merely a new approach but a new subject in its own right. Encouraged by his report, I proceeded to Leeds University where I completed a doctoral thesis under the title *The Study of Ecclesiastical Administration using the Methods and Insights of Public Administration*. The thesis eventually became something more than the mere application of principles of public administration to the ecclesiastical sphere: it involved a study of organizational theory, which is anterior to all administrative studies, and the finding of the theory that was most consonant with the fundamentals of theology. And so the final product was a real marrying of two diverse disciplines, the tying together of the two main threads of my life.

I have persisted in using the name 'ecclesiastical administration'; I say 'persisted' because it has been in the face of contrary advice and in spite of many misunderstandings of the meaning of administration, not least in church circles. Nevertheless, I have always seen administration as having a rightful dignity and I have desired that this particular study should stand alongside the established and emerging administrative disciplines.

However, it may be helpful to some people to think of the subject by an alternative name, 'managerial theology'. It is of the same status as other branches of applied theology and shares their character. For instance, liturgical theology involves the taking of the basic doctrines of dogmatic theology and the finding of their expression in liturgical form. In the same way, managerial theology has its basis in fundamental Christian dogmas and is concerned with their counterparts in organization and administration.

The fact that these terms had to be coined is some indication of the novelty of the subject, but I should not leave the impression that this has been a lone effort, even though I must take responsibility for the form in which it is presented. Many, many people have contributed to the development of this subject and to them I express my gratitude.

I have mentioned some of the pioneers in the first two chapters; I have quoted from the works of a number of authors and I am grateful to them and to their publishers for the use of the material; I have referred to many other authors in the text and the bibliography; and I have drawn on still others. It would be too lengthy a process to recall by name all who have helped me in my work: in respect of the Leeds thesis alone, I listed some 125 people and fifty institutions that had afforded me valuable assistance; and there have been many in earlier years and in more recent times who have had faith in the possibilities of this project. My thanks go out to them all and I trust that the publication of this work will bring them a real sense of satisfaction.

It may be possible in the future to be more specific in my acknowledgements. In the course of research, I have had unique opportunities of access to many unpublished documents, reports, and theses; and should it be possible to publish these in due course in the form of a reader in ecclesiastical administration, the nature of my debt to others would be apparent. Such documentation would give support and fullness to the presentation which I have tried to set out here in a brief and succinct way.

P. F. R.

Canberra, Australia
July 1968

ACKNOWLEDGEMENTS

For permission to quote extracts from published and unpublished works thanks are due to the following:

George Allen & Unwin Ltd, London, in respect of *Social Policy and Administration* by D. V. Donnison and others; The Anglican Church of Canada, Toronto, in respect of the *Journal of Proceedings of General Synod*; Association Press, New York, in respect of *Our Changing Churches: A Study of Leadership* by Joseph Van Vleck Jr; the Editor of *Church Management* and C. Russell Stout in respect of 'Manse or Living Allowance'; the Editor of the *Seminary Quarterly* and Ross P. Scherer in respect of 'The Ministry and its Sources of Income'; First Presbyterian Church, Fort Wayne, Indiana, in respect of *A Handbook to Help Acquaint You with First Presbyterian Church*; The Free Press, a division of The Macmillan Company, in respect of *The Theory of Social and Economic Organization* by Max Weber; Harper & Row, Publishers, Inc., New York, in respect of *Christ and Culture* and *The Purpose of the Church and its Ministry* by H. Richard Niebuhr; Helicon Press Inc., Baltimore, and Helicon Limited, Dublin, in respect of *Change and the Catholic Church* by Jeremiah Newman; Hodder & Stoughton Limited, London, in respect of *Beauty and Bands* by Kenneth E. Kirk, *Cosmo Gordon Lang* by J. G. Lockhart, and *Cyril Forster Garbett* by Charles Smyth; McGraw-Hill Book Company, New York, in respect of *The Human Side of Enterprise* by Douglas McGregor; Oxford University Press, London, in respect of *Randall Davidson: Archbishop of Canterbury* by G. K. A. Bell, and *William Temple: Archbishop of Canterbury* by F. A. Iremonger; Presbyterian Bookroom, Christchurch, NZ, in respect of *Training for the Ministry* by Richard H. T. Thompson; Price Waterhouse & Co., Vancouver, in respect of *The Anglican Church of Canada in the Diocese of Rupert's Land*; The Seabury Press, New York, in respect of *Beauty and Bands* by Kenneth E. Kirk; John H. Simpson in respect of *A Study of the Role of the Protestant Parish Minister with special reference to Organization Theory*; SPCK, London, in respect of *The Parish Priest at Work* by Charles R. Forder; Tavistock Publications Limited, in respect of *The Management of Innovation* by Tom Burns and G. M. Stalker; University of Notre Dame Press, South Bend, Indiana, in respect of *Religion as an Occupation* by Joseph H. Fichter; The Westminster Press, Philadelphia, and Lutterworth Press, London, in respect of *Images of the Church in the New Testament* by Paul S. Minear.

The following permissions in respect of unpublished documents are also acknowledged with thanks:

The Rt Rev. J. R. H. Moorman, Lord Bishop of Ripon, in respect of *A History of the Diocese of Ripon 1936–66* (embodied in Rudge, 1966a); the Rev. A. N. Thomas, Vicar of Seacroft, in respect of *The Parish of Seacroft: A New Creation* (Rudge, 1966b).

PART ONE

The Development of Ecclesiastical Administration

CHAPTER I

Diverse Administrative Studies

The theme of this book is the development of ecclesiastical administration. But what is meant by this term?

One way of understanding what is implied is to consider ecclesiastical administration as one of a number of diverse administrative studies such as public administration, social administration, and business administration. It is the body of administrative knowledge appropriate to religious bodies in the same way that public administration pertains to governmental activities, that social administration is proper to welfare services, and that business administration is related to commercial and industrial enterprises.

A notable feature of recent decades has been the development of these varied studies, to which others may now be added. Thus it is possible to study on the academic level the administration of schools or hospitals; and management is becoming a serious concern in occupations ranging from engineering to farming.

In this growing list of administrative studies, it is proposed that a further study be included, namely, ecclesiastical administration. It may be somewhat novel to think of this as one of many diverse administrative studies; but in fact the subject itself is not new. There have been some important developments in the past of which note will be taken. However, the history may be made more intelligible by reference to a besetting problem of all administrative studies.

The term 'administration' is often very limited in its meaning: it can refer to mundane office routine and paper-work. In a university, for instance, there may be different buildings for the various departments and another building labelled 'Administration'. The work of lecturing and research goes on in the departments and this is regarded as the real function of the university; by comparison, the activities in the administrative building are considered as being inferior and dull.

To limit administrative studies to the latter kind of work is to reduce them to a secondary status and to take them out of the context which gives them their full meaning and significance. One of the most vigorous protests against this narrow view of administration was that by D. V. Donnison and his colleagues in the book *Social Policy and Administration* (1965, pp. 40–1):

> In common parlance the word 'administration' often refers to a special form of work which may be contrasted with other kinds of work – with 'policy making' or 'professional work' for example. Though this usage may be convenient for distinguishing different aspects of the administrative process and the capacities required at different points in an administrative hierarchy, it too often restricts and confuses the questions the serious student of the subject should be asking. 'Administration', for him, should include *all* the activities and influences that determine the character and outcome of the tasks he is studying. He is interested in *all* who participate in these processes and contribute to their outcome – whether or not they happen to be called 'administrators', and whether or not they are employed by the agency whose work he is studying.

Thus the student of social administration is not primarily concerned with the designing and filling in of forms but with the total provision of social welfare. Likewise, public administration is not so much about how a junior clerk sticks on stamps or files away papers but about the whole character of a government ministry. This wide meaning is retained in such expressions as the Kennedy or Johnson administration in the United States and the Conservative or Labour administration in England.

The far-reaching connotation is essential to the understanding of ecclesiastical administration; in fact, this meaning is deeply embedded in church life. The word 'administration' is derived from the same root as is 'ministry' and it is used in reference to sacred things as in the phrase 'the administration of the sacraments'. Petition is made in the Anglican ember prayer for 'all those who are to be called to any office and administration' in the church; during the absence of a bishop or the vacancy of a see, the person in charge is called the administrator; and when Archbishop Ramsey was elected to the see of Canterbury, the dean called for 'hearty prayer for His Grace's long life and happy administration'. This prayer was more than a hope that the archbishop might enjoy his office work: it was a concern for the leadership that the new primate might give to the church.

THE ENGLISH SCENE

Nevertheless, the narrow view of administration has generally prevailed in English ecclesiastical circles: this aspect of church life has been disparaged; the development of the serious study of ecclesiastical administration has been stultified; and churchmen have been very reluctant to take any interest at all.

The administrative side has been seen in opposition to the pastoral; the one is despised, the other regarded as the essence of the ministry. In the training of clergy, only the latter has been taken seriously; it has been felt that it was sufficient to prepare men for the various pastoral roles that they would be called on to perform: preaching, conducting services, visiting, counselling, teaching. Very little has been done in theological colleges to prepare men for their administrative work or, in the wider sense, for their future charge as incumbents of a parish; Anthony P. M. Coxon (1965, p. 521), for instance, has shown that Anglican ordinands have been over-trained for the roles of father, priest, preacher, and pastor, and under-prepared for those of parson, rector, and cleric.

An alternative view to the antithesis of the administrative and the pastoral is that taken by Charles R. Forder in *The Parish Priest at Work* (1947) – almost a lone voice which stressed that the administrative side should be considered in a positive way as a necessary aspect of a priest's work. Forder stated (p. 5) that the aim of parochial administration 'is to plan and organize the time and activities of the parochial clergy, and the various affairs of the parish, in such a way as to obtain in practice a maximum of efficiency, saving of time, and the elimination of friction'. He went on to say that 'so only will the clergy be as free as possible for devotion, study, and evangelism'. In the light of this principle he wrote what was virtually a handbook about every aspect of parish life. It was first published in 1947 and a second edition appeared in 1959; it was widely circulated but perhaps seldom used; the point of view has not been generally accepted in church circles.

However, the pressure of administrative work has remained as a reality in life; bishops in particular have become conscious of their administrative burdens, and they have been criticized for such preoccupations. Some account has had to be taken of administrative phenomena, and various attempts have been made to come to grips with the problem in theological terms. One of the most notable was the sermon by Kenneth E. Kirk, subsequently published under the title *Beauty and Bands* (1955). He wrestled with the conflict between the 'beauty' of the pastoral ministry and the 'bands' of administrative duties; and he tried to find a resolution of the tension by showing how the Christian approach to administration could enrich it with personal concerns, with pastoral perspectives, and with opportunities for intimate care. Thus the administrative activities were but another opening for the exercise of the ministry. Kirk had as his guide his predecessor in the diocese of Oxford, Samuel Wilberforce, of whom he wrote in these words (p. 15):

> He accepted the bands of organisation and administration as an integral part of his pastoral ministry, and those who heard him were as much moved when he spoke to them in the Conference chamber as when he proclaimed the word of God from the pulpit of his Cathedral. He thought of his committee work and correspondence not as a hindrance to direct pastoral activity, but as its essential concomitant.

This was an attractive and visionary attempt to grapple with the issue; and it is perhaps the best answer to the problem set in dichotomous terms. However, there is still the common English assumption that administration is to be disparaged, though in this answer an attempt is made to rescue it from being maligned and to infuse it with some better quality. The limited answer is a reflection of the limited conception of the problem: only two functions are assumed – the pastoral and the administrative – whereas it will be shown later that there is a third – the monitoring – in the light of which the two find their rightful place, relationship, and dignity.

Such thinking arises from the proper study of the subject of ecclesiastical administration, the development of which has been precluded in the English scene by the general reluctance to countenance it. However, there have been a number of signs of a change in attitude, particularly in the 1960s.

For instance, the Rev. G. Stuart Snell was appointed in 1964 as a Fellow of St Augustine's College with a view to his pursuing administrative studies; and one of his ventures was to sponsor a conference on church administration in the September of that year. The idea of a staff college for the Church of England was mooted by John Adair in an article in *Theology* (1962, pp. 194–7); the recommended course was the comprehensive study of ecclesiastical administration. On somewhat similar lines to this proposal has been the founding of St George's House, which was opened at Windsor in 1966.

The publication in 1964 of Leslie Paul's report, *The Deployment and Payment of the Clergy*, provoked considerable discussion about the personnel policy of the Church of England, and churchmen became more conscious of administrative issues; the report was followed by a further investigation of the same topic. Another commission was charged by the Archbishop of Canterbury to consider the organization of the Church of England in the South-East of England.

Among the many other factors that have conspired to focus interest in this field of study have been the development of professional fund-raising, the proposals for union between the Church of England and the Methodist Church, the widespread interest in group dynamics, and the attempts to form team and group ministries.

Expressive of the growing interest has been the spate of popular books about parish life, particularly with reference to novel and experimental ministries. Some of the interest has been focused on the activities and publications of the movement called 'Parish and People'; and the periodicals *Prism* and its successor *New Christian* have been used as a forum for the discussion of administrative issues. Another indication has been the appointment of lay administrators in several parishes; and a few parishes, dioceses, and church organizations have engaged professional consultants to advise them on some of their problems.

One further development is related to ecclesiastical biography. Kirk referred to the life of his predecessor to illustrate the point he was making about the relation of the pastoral and the administrative; and there has been a growing awareness of the potential value of such literature in providing source material about the administrative behaviour of church leaders.

These instances perhaps indicate that the traditional English reluctance, particularly in church circles, to countenance administrative studies is disappearing.

THE NORTH AMERICAN SITUATION

By contrast, there has been little reluctance in this respect in the church in North America (both the United States and Canada); rather, there has been a willingness to discuss administrative issues and an eagerness to establish an appropriate body of knowledge. The subject of pastoral administration is recognized alongside its counterparts in other areas of concern such as business and government; the development of an administrative study appropriate to voluntary and community bodies is also a feature of North American life.

One of the earliest books in the ecclesiastical field was Don Frank Denn's *Parish Administration*, published in 1938. This has been followed by other handbooks on the subject, such as Andrew W. Blackwood, *Pastoral Leadership*, in 1949, and, more recently, William H. Leach, *Handbook of Church Management* (1958), Gaines S. Dobbins, *The Ministering Church* (1960), Lowell Russell Ditzen, *Handbook of Church Administration* (1962), Arthur Merrihew Adams, *Pastoral Administration* (1964). In addition, there are many other books on more specific topics such as stewardship, group leadership, and personnel management; and there are at least two periodicals devoted to the general field: *Church Administration* and *Church Management*.

This literature, besides embodying the knowledge on ecclesiastical administration, forms the basis of courses for the training of clergy. The role of administrator is recognized as an essential part of the ministry, and men are prepared for the exercise of this function. In many divinity schools, there are courses on parish administration; in some cases there are faculties and professors whose special interest lies in this field. The emphasis is mainly on the practical aspect of parish life; and the lectures and handbooks are designed with this in view.

Beyond the pre-ordination training, there are courses in church administration at various levels. For instance, the Center of Continuing Education at the Princeton Theological Seminary caters for the needs of men whose ministry is normally to local congregations. A more specialized training is provided for those who wish to serve in œcumenical work on councils of churches; for a number of years such courses have been given in the Institute on Ecumenical Leadership in the Boston University summer term. For church executives on the highest level, very intensive courses have been planned and carried out by the Church Executive Development Board of the National Council of the Churches of Christ.

Another significant American development has been the extent to which full-time lay administrators have been appointed in local churches. The number of such officers in the United States is probably over one thousand, about half of whom belong to a professional association called the National Association of Church Business Administrators. The association adopted its constitution in 1957 and has met regularly since then. Among its aims are the provision of professional training, the setting of business standards, and the certification of members whose competence has been demonstrated.

It is not uncommon in Canada as well as in the United States for churches, particularly on the diocesan and national level, to engage management consultants to assist them with their organizational problems. The consultants generally have shown a remarkable sensitivity to the character of their assignments, respecting the theological nature of the church, the conception of its purpose (as distinct from that of business organizations), and the involvement and commitment of the members. Their reports deserve a wider publicity because they would add appreciably to the growing body of knowledge about church organization.

Advisory services to churches are also provided by various units of sociological and demographic research such as Church Surveys in Boston University School of Theology and the General Division of Research and Field Study in the Episcopal Church Center, New York. The recommendations in their studies imply a knowledge of ecclesiastical administration.

This subject, then, is more consciously developed and accepted in North America than in England; but in both countries there is a common feature in that the interest is primarily practical. The concern of the practitioner is uppermost: the books, the courses, the reports, are all directed to the needs of the person in the active ministry who is facing administrative problems. For this reason, the subject generally tends to lack the academic standing and the theoretical refinement to which many of the other administrative studies have attained. Nevertheless, it is coming to be recognized as having a place alongside them.

CHAPTER 2

Common Organizational Theory

In the first chapter, concern was with ecclesiastical administration as distinct from public or social or business administration. Yet these several studies share the same title 'administration'. What is the common element that is implied in this word? And can the subject of ecclesiastical administration be developed in the light of what belongs to all administrative fields?

It is recognized that there is a body of knowledge anterior to all areas of administrative study, which may be called 'administrative science' or 'organizational theory'. This is the common element underlying all such disciplines be they concerned with school or government or hospital or business enterprise. One who has recognized this point is Adair who, in a recent book *Training for Leadership* (1968), put forward a concept of the functions of a leader and showed how it could be used for the analysis and illumination of the offices of a teacher, an army officer, a minister, and other persons in authority.

In some fields the underlying theory has been very prominent. In public administration, the publication of Herbert A. Simon's *Administrative Behavior* in 1948 was an important milestone; this was 'A Study of the Decision-making Processes in Administrative Organization', according to the subtitle. It was followed in 1950 by *Public Administration* (Simon, Smithburg, and Thompson). In these works, a theory of decision-making was evolved that is applicable to all kinds of organizations, although in the second book it is expressed in a way that is appropriate to governmental activities.

In business administration, there has been a basic concern for the fundamental theory. For instance, J. D. Mooney and A. C. Reiley, in a pioneering book called *Onward Industry!* (1931), based their exposition on the classical theory of management in which the organization is seen in mechanistic terms (this and other theories are explained fully in the next chapter); they saw that this theory underlay such diverse institutions as the army and the Roman Catholic Church as well as business undertakings. The alternative theory deriving from the human relations approach, in which the stress is on the personal elements in an organization, sprang out of the original work by Elton Mayo (1933); a sophisticated version of it is seen in the development of group dynamics. More recently, other management writers such as Tom Burns and G. M. Stalker (1961) have attempted to formulate a theory based on the conception of an organization as an organism or a system. Thus there has been a strong theoretical element in the growth of business administration.

However, in the field of social administration, the awareness of the common organizational theory came at a later stage. For many years, the approach had been descriptive – of the history of social welfare, of the laws governing the provision of services, of the practices of administrators. One of the first attempts at studying social administration in the light of common organizational theory was the book by Donnison *et al.* (1965). By means of case-studies, they examined a number of situations in which social administrators worked, and found that two of the commonly known modes of operation – the classical and the human relations – were not adequate to explain the phenomena. They looked for a theory of management that would be a guide to the providers of social services; in doing so, they realized the need for a theory on the lines of the systemic, in order to allow for great flexibility of operation in pursuing the goal of 'welfare', which could not be precisely defined. In this way, they sought to build up their particular administrative study by reference to the common body of knowledge that underlies all such fields.

This theoretical work has been elaborated in its own right. One of the founders was Max Weber, who, in *The Theory of Social and Economic Organization* (1947), set forth his three types of legitimate authority: the traditional, the charismatic, and the bureaucratic (the charismatic is based on the intuitive recognition of a magnetic quality in the personality of the leader). Weber produced illustrations from many kinds of organizations. The scholar who has specialized in this field in more recent times has been Amitai Etzioni whose notable work, *A Comparative Analysis of Complex Organizations*, was published in 1961. Here he devised a typology by which all organizations could be classified according to his criteria of 'compliance' – the relationship of the leader and the led. Organizations range from the authoritarian (involving extreme coercion by the leader with great resistance on the part of members) to the utilitarian (moderate degrees of direction and co-operation) to the normative (little direction but complete commitment by the members).

The importance of the organizational theory formulated by such writers as these is that churches were included in the general analysis. Thus, in Weber's terms, religious bodies could have features corresponding to his three types; Etzioni classified churches as belonging to the normative type of organization because they depended very considerably on full and free participation by their members. Such thinking paved the way for those who were specially interested in churches to develop the study of ecclesiastical administration in the light of the underlying organizational theory.

A pioneer work in this field had been that by Joseph Van Vleck (1937), entitled *Our Changing Churches: A Study of Leadership*. He realized (p. 113) that 'church leaders either consciously or unconsciously must make premises upon the probable religious conduct of their constituencies to guide them in plan making and in program and pastoral activities'. To enable these basic assumptions to be uncovered and examined, he put forward a threefold typology: priestly, individualist, and democratic. These modes of operation corresponded roughly to the Catholic, Protestant, and conciliar elements in Christianity; they were also counterparts to the traditional, charismatic, and human relations theories of management. Van Vleck showed that the administrative behaviour of ministers tended to follow one or other of these ways even though ministers themselves were not always conscious of this.

His inquiry had a further importance in that he tried to reveal how these patterns of operation were based on theological presuppositions of which the ministers themselves might not be aware. He observed (p. 105): 'Often a minister is so convinced of the divine nature of the pattern he employs that he does not realize it rests upon certain assumptions about human nature that may no longer be valid.' He showed that the priestly approach involved an emphasis on the doctrines of the will of God, the mediatorial role of the priest, heaven and hell, the importance of the church, and the unimportance of this world. The individualist stressed personal experience, the freedom of the individual contrasted with the authority of the church, and the influence of rewards and punishment upon behaviour. Typical of the democratic way was that 'God is approached through sharing any form of truth, goodness or beauty as well as through the church or mysticism or conversion' (p. 107); there was little emphasis on the next world; service to mankind in promoting human happiness was the goal in life. These were the respective theological positions that underlay the various modes of administrative behaviour that ministers adopted.

In subsequent attempts to evolve theories of ecclesiastical administration, the doctrinal basis has been virtually neglected and the main interest has been in the potential value of management and sociological schemes of analysis.

Thus E. K. Francis (1950, pp. 437–49) examined the character of the various religious orders down through history and noted that the trend was capable of being expressed in terms of the fundamental sociological distinction between *Gemeinschaft* and *Gesellschaft*. These were the terms used by the German scholar Ferdinand Tönnies (1955) to portray the distinction between two types of organization. The former was the natural community in which people were born and brought up, a community that had an organic quality about it; by contrast, the latter type was a rationally constructed organization based on deliberate choice and contractual relationships. Francis showed that early monasticism had the familial quality of the first category; but in the course of history there was a move towards the second type, notably seen in the highly rationalized Jesuit order.

To a considerable extent, the distinction is reproduced in Weber's typology: the traditional roughly corresponds to *Gemeinschaft*; the bureaucratic to *Gesellschaft*. The charismatic makes up the threefold typology; and sociologists of religion such as David O. Moberg (1962, pp. 95–8) have recognized that the Weberian scheme has relevance to the study of religious bodies. Paul M. Harrison modified the typology for use in the analysis of voluntary bodies (1960, pp. 232–7; 1965), and he used it in his examination of the American Baptist Convention (1959). Likewise, D. H. J. Morgan, in his study of English diocesan bishops (1963), noted that their administrative behaviour generally followed the traditional pattern and an institutionalized form of the charismatic, and that this character had persisted in spite of the development of features in the church on the lines of the bureaucratic theory.

The Weberian bureaucratic category was a progenitor of the classical theory of management. One of the exponents of this theory was Chester I. Barnard in *The Functions of the Executive* (1938). This book was the starting-point for one of the most profound attempts to use management studies in relation to religious bodies. John H. Simpson virtually transposed the whole book into an ecclesiastical setting in his thesis *A Study of the Role of the Protestant Parish Minister with special reference to Organization Theory* (1965). He was able to do this primarily because he recognized more clearly than did most ecclesiastical writers that the position of a parish minister was comparable with that of an executive; he said (p. 100): 'the most useful way of viewing the overall function of the minister is to consider him as the chief executive of the local congregation who may spend a large amount of time performing specific professional tasks'. The guidelines for management set out by Barnard could therefore be transferred to help the minister in his work – for example, the importance of finding the 'strategic' factor in an organization and concentrating action at that point.

The Roman Catholic Church has often been regarded as an ideal illustration of the classical theory of management; in fact, early management writers such as Mooney and Reiley (1931) drew many of their illustrations from the structure of that church. A Roman Catholic sociologist, A. E. C. W. Spencer, has used concepts from classical theory to analyse the structure of his church from the level of the papacy to the level of the parish. In his paper, 'The Span of Control, Scalar Development and the Structure of the Church's Administration' (1963), he drew attention to the need for the establishment of deanery, national, and continental levels of organization, thereby reducing 'the span of control' but lengthening 'the chain of command' between the papacy and the parish. More recently (1966), he attempted to use the management theory of Rensis Likert (1961) to describe developments and to solve problems associated with the second Vatican Council and the apparent ferment of opinion in the church. Likert's distinction between authoritative and participative decision-making proved to be an illuminating concept in studying the conciliar movement.

The latter distinction is but one of the many points of contrast between the classical and human relations theories of management. Churchmen have often felt dissatisfied with the mechanistic element of the classical theory and in consequence have preferred the personal emphasis in the human relations theory. Thus the National Council of Churches in New York produced a document (n.d.) giving expression to this preference; it included the following points:

1. Wide participation in decision-making rather than centralized decision-making.

2. The face-to-face group, rather than the individual, as the basic unit of the organization.
3. Mutual confidence, rather than authority, as the integrative force in organization.
4. The supervisor as the agent for maintaining intragroup and intergroup communication rather than the agent of higher authority.
5. Growth of members of the organization to greater responsibility, rather than external control of members' performance of their tasks.

The Church of England Board of Education in London also issued papers (1965) setting out similar contrasts in organizational approaches; and the distinction between the authoritarian and democratic ways was a fundamental feature in the works of the French writer, Marcel Ducos, O.P., about the church in his own country (1963).

An alternative to emphasizing the antithesis of the classical and human relations theories has been the attempt to find a midway position between them. Harrison (1960, pp. 232–7; 1965) did this when he devised the category called 'rational-pragmatic', which was a modification of the classical theory to suit the nature of voluntary bodies. D. A. Martin (1962, p. 6) also used the term 'pragmatic' to describe the decision-making process in the denominational type of religious organization; and it is perhaps the position attained by many American writers on ecclesiastical administration. They have approached the subject from the practical angle; and the test of any method of procedure has been whether it was workable or not. That is, the standard has been essentially pragmatic; but this stance can be analysed in theoretical terms as the reorienting of the basic classical position in the light of the personal nature of the organizations with which they have been concerned.

Another significant contribution was that of Joesph H. Fichter who saw, in his book *Religion as an Occupation* (1961, p. 256), that 'in spite of certain differences, the leadership role in religious groups is roughly synonymous with that of management and administration in non-ecclesiastical organizations'. He went on to discuss the 'executive functions of superiors' (pp. 255–79) and set out a typology closely related to management theory (pp. 211–33). He suggested three types of organization: the familial, the bureaucratic, and the professional (similar to the systemic); and then spelt out more specifically the contrasts between the last two. His chart (p. 224) was as follows:

Bureaucratic mode of organization requires	*Professional mode of organization requires*
Centralized leadership	Leadership of expertness
Emphasis on procedure	Variability of procedures
Simplification of tasks	Totality of tasks
Little initiative	Broad initiative
Corporate responsibility	Personal responsibility
Impersonal relations	Close colleague relations
Ascribed status	Achieved status
Service to system	Service to clients

Fichter's chart has the value of showing that the alternative theoretical approaches can be translated into detailed points about the nature of the administrative process and that these points can differ very considerably from theory to theory.

This kind of development has been pressed even further by Ross P. Scherer (1964, 1965a, 1965b), who was concerned with the personnel management of clergy in the United States. He took over the various theories of organization and showed how these had a considerable bearing on such matters as methods of payment. He devised the following parallelism (1965a, p. 1) to show the contrasting features of remuneration policies corresponding to two alternative approaches:

Patrimonial-Patronage	*Bureaucratic*
Personal	Impersonal
Particular	Universal
Locally controlled	Centralized
Multiple sources of income	Single salary source
Non-standardized, sporadic	Regularized, scaled
Traditional, ceremonial	Purposefully rational
Fusion of public and private spheres of life	Separation of public and private

The first pattern, similar to the traditional, is common in the Church of England where a minister receives a benefice income which may vary from parish to parish, further cash payments as an augmentation, fees for various services, perhaps an allowance for expenses of office, maybe rent from glebe lands, the use of a vicarage, and often gifts in kind especially in the country. The second scheme is more closely related to the methods of clergy payment that prevail in at least some churches in North America, whereby a regularized scale of remuneration is paid from a central fund in one cash sum to cover all needs, including housing. Besides illuminating this distinction, Scherer's statement has an importance on the theoretical level by showing that the smallest details of administration (in the limited sense of that word) are related to the general character of the pattern of management.

The general character of such patterns, together with their corresponding detailed features, constitutes the body of knowledge called organizational theory which is common to all administrative studies. The study of ecclesiastical administration has been advanced considerably, particularly by social scientists, through drawing upon this common stock. The next step is to do this more comprehensively and to link the various organizational approaches, as Van Vleck (1937) attempted to do, with the theology that characterizes the bodies with which ecclesiastical administration, as distinct from other administrative studies, is concerned.

PART TWO

The Theory of Ecclesiastical Administration

CHAPTER 3

The Theory in Organizational Terms

The foregoing chapter has served as an introduction to the kind of thinking that is embodied in organizational theory; the purpose of the present chapter is to spell out clearly and succinctly the full content of this body of knowledge so as to lay the foundations of the theory of ecclesiastical administration.

In brief, there are five main ways in which an organization may be operated; alternatively, there are five theories of management in terms of which organizational behaviour may be described and understood.

The names of the theories may vary, but the preferred titles are:

Traditional
Charismatic
Classical
Human relations
Systemic

The traditional may sometimes be called the 'patrimonial', and it corresponds roughly to the German *Gemeinschaft*.

For the general reader, the epithet 'intuitive' might be more meaningful than 'charismatic', but the latter term is retained because of its familiarity in theological and sociological circles. Its appropriateness as a title has been challenged by writers of Marxist persuasion who reject the attributing of the kind of behaviour concerned to superhuman sources, as Weber (1947, pp. 358–63) does; Peter Worsley (1957, pp. 257–76), for instance, associated such behaviour with social and economic conditions of upheaval and unrest. The formulation of a separate theory of this name has been questioned by such writers as Etzioni (1961), who showed that there was a charismatic element in other types of leadership. However, the name and theory are preserved in this work because there is a distinguishable administrative and decision-making process appropriate to them.

'Bureaucratic' was Weber's term for the classical theory; but the word has unfortunately acquired overtones which tend to bring discredit on the theory. Instead, the title 'classical' is preferred because it avoids the pejorative element and also gives the theory credit for its long history and dominant position in organizational thinking. Alternatively the theory might be called 'mechanistic'; and it corresponds generally to the term *Gesellschaft*. An interesting observation is that this theory is commonly given the name of 'traditional' in America; this is an indication of the extent to which this theory is deeply rooted in the highly conscious development of organizational thinking there and of the difference between the American and the English starting-points. Nevertheless, in this book the traditional implies the patrimonial and is never used for the mechanistic or classical theory.

The human relations theory might also be called the 'group' theory when the group is the basic unit of organization. On the other hand, the organization may be more like a public association than an intimate group; it may be highly structured and constitutionally evolved; furthermore, it is possible in such a body for the decision-making to be participative in character and for the impetus in organizational life to come from its members – in which case the term 'democratic' is more appropriate than 'group' or even than the chosen title 'human relations'. Nevertheless, it is the human relations theory that is expounded although, when suitable, the alternative name of 'democratic' is used.

The term 'systemic' is derived from the word system, but the theory concerned should not be called the 'systematic', an epithet which applies more accurately to the classical theory. Sometimes the synonyms of 'organic' or 'organismic' are used, but the preferred title means that the theory is removed from too close connections with biological models. The professional type of organization outlined by Fichter (1961, p. 224) is similar to the systemic, and such a title could possibly be used.

In the chart in which the several theories are summarized (pp. 32–3), various symbols are used; they are convenient for reference purposes. The traditional is called 'Theory A' because it is characteristic of organizations at the beginning of their natural history. The initial letter of charismatic supplies the symbol for that theory. 'X' and 'Y' are borrowed from the important work by Douglas McGregor (1960) on the classical and human relations theories. The systemic is called 'Theory Z' simply because it was conceived after Theories X and Y, though it must not be confused with attempts by such writers as W. J. Reddin (1964, pp. 9–18) to add a 'Z' dimension to the earlier theories nor taken to mean that it is necessarily the last word in management theory.

The approaches to organizational life that are expressed in the several theories bearing the above names and symbols can be summed up in convenient and precise phrases. Thus the focus of the traditional theory is on 'maintaining a tradition'; the essential features of the other theories are expressed in corresponding phrases:

Traditional – maintaining a tradition
Charismatic – pursuing an intuition
Classical – running a machine
Human relations – leading groups
Systemic – adapting a system

The exposition of these theories is virtually the drawing out of the implications of these epigrams in relation to a number of points, such as the conception of the organization, the nature of the decision-making process, and the function of the leader. In this way, the nature of the respective administrative processes will be revealed.

The traditional theory

In the traditional theory, an organization is envisaged which has a continuing life of its own, and from within it there is a momentum which keeps it going; at the same time, there are forces which ensure that in its continuance it follows the same path as before. The organization is a historical institution which has existed for many years in the past and for which there is every prospect of an unchanging course in the future.

Less obvious than its historic continuance, though just as important, is the coherence of the organization: it has a wholeness; it has parts which are held together by virtue of their inherence in the continuing whole; and the pattern of their interrelationship is undisturbed and unexplicit. The term 'unexplicit' is used because it means more than 'implicit'; it suggests that the relationship can be made explicit but in fact has not been, because such a level of consciousness has not been reached in the kind of organization that is envisaged.

The organization, although it has a wholeness of its own, is itself a part of a wider society, a culture that is static and unchanging. It is embedded in its environment, and its character is completely attuned to that of its surrounds.

The leader has his place among the elite of elders, the wise, and the sacred; his task is implicit in the phrase 'maintaining a tradition'. He is not the initiator of tradition but rather the embodiment of it, the living example and expression of it. He is the fount of wisdom; he expounds what the tradition is; he nurtures people in it; he encourages them to follow in its pattern; he protects it against deviations.

Decision-making is virtually a continuous process whereby the tradition is maintained. It is non-reflective; there is no need to reflect because there is no alternative to choosing again what has been done before. Apart from the day-to-day matters, there are the major recurring decisions about the great ceremonial occasions which provide the focal points of traditional culture. These decisions are also non-reflective but they are made explicit by the announcement of the leader.

There is some communication, but there is little need for it, since the tradition is shared and known by all, and each has his part to play; the main direction of communication is to those who are being brought up in the tradition. Consent to decisions is unexplicit; reaction is explicit only when there is an attempt to break with an accepted custom. Therein lies some indication of the process of control; but there is little need for its exercise because of the lack of awareness of any alternative courses of action.

As well as giving the name to this theory, Weber expounded the foundation on which it rested; he said (1947, p. 341):

> a system of imperative authority will be called 'traditional' if legitimacy is claimed for it and believed in on the basis of the sanctity of the order and the attendant powers of control as they have been handed down from the past, 'have always existed'. The person or persons exercising authority are designated according to traditionally transmitted rules. The object of obedience is the personal authority of the individual which he enjoys by virtue of his traditional status. The organized group exercising authority is, in the simplest case, primarily based on relations of personal loyalty, cultivated through a common process of education. The person exercising authority is not a 'superior', but a personal 'chief'.

This conception of authority is basic to the traditional theory, and all the other points of the theory – the shape of the organization, the decision-making process, the role of the leader – are derived from it.

The charismatic theory

A charismatic leader is typified as one who 'pursues an intuition'. An intuition is sometimes in the form of an inspiration, a flash of enlightenment, or a revelation; or it may be the expression of a mere whim or fancy. A charismatic leader is one who has this kind of perception and who acts upon what is thus perceived.

The leader announces, usually by the spoken word, the content of the intuition to all; and those who recognize, again by intuition, that his words have a compelling and magnetic quality become his followers and join with him in fulfilling the content of the message. Both he and they are bound to obedience and complete support of the goals made explicit in his utterance. The decision-making process is thus an instantaneous perception, and the outcome is announced in definitive and discrete terms by the leader, the followers according their support at least while they continue to recognize the intuitive element in the leader.

What organization there is has focus in the intuition. It is a gathered community of the enlightened who draw their inspiration from the prophetic leader; all parts of the organization adhere to him as pieces of metal to a magnet; any further structure is on a temporary basis for the accomplishment of the particular purposes indicated in the message and it has no significance or even existence beyond that.

Implicit is the rejection of all other existing organizations. The charismatic approach involves cutting at the roots of the past, overthrowing formalism, and launching out afresh. The approach thus has a flexibility by which to meet new situations: it can articulate the forces in social change, and so it can be closely attuned to the environment, although this is not necessarily true of all intuitions.

The judgemental qualities of the prophetic message provide a control process within the whole organization: all members, all procedures, all structures, are subject to its searching scrutiny. The leader himself, being the person who voices the intuition, may appear to be setting his own standards and so to be free from control; but control is exercised over him by virtue of the fact that his adherents can withdraw their support when they perceive that he no longer has the authority of the charisma.

This last point was at the basis of Weber's consideration of the legitimation of this type of authority; he said (pp. 358–9):

> the term 'charisma' will be applied to a certain quality of an individual personality by virtue of which he is set apart from ordinary men and treated as endowed with supernatural, superhuman, or at least specifically exceptional powers or qualities. These are such as are not accessible to the ordinary person, but are regarded as of divine origin or as exemplary, and on the basis of them the individual concerned is treated as a leader. . . . What is alone important is how the individual is actually regarded by those subject to charismatic authority, by his 'followers' or 'disciples'.

He thus focused attention on the nature of compliance in this theory of organization.

The classical theory

The classical theory is constructed around the dominant theme of 'running a machine'. The organization is conceived as a mechanistic structure on the lines of a pyramidal organization chart. Each part is distinct from the others; but each is linked in a vertical direction until the apex of the pyramid is reached. The person at the top is the vital figure in the organization since its activity depends on his initiative and drive. Everything is under his direct control from the point of original impetus to the final check on all the parts to see that each has performed its appointed task. The objective is to maximize the efficiency of the machine so that the task is performed most effectively. The task is expressed in precise quantitative terms; the decision-making process consists of a series of highly rationalized steps; the decisions are expressed as orders which are issued to the subordinates. The members of the organization are subject to coercion; their response is that of obedience to instructions, and it springs from their recognition of the legal authority of the superior or from their contractual relationship with him.

This theory was given its earliest expression in Weber's ideal type of bureaucracy; and since then it has been expounded by a number of writers over a sufficiently long period for it to be known as the classical theory of organization. Another exponent of note was L. Urwick (1944), who developed it as a series of principles of organization. The characteristics of this approach were listed by Burns and Stalker (1961), and their description is quoted below because it prepared the way for a valuable comparison with the systemic theory which these authors did so much to promote. They said (pp. 119–20):

A *mechanistic* management system is appropriate to stable conditions. It is characterized by:

(a) the specialized differentiation of functional tasks into which the problems and tasks facing the concern as a whole are broken down;
(b) the abstract nature of each individual task, which is pursued with techniques and purposes more or less distinct from those of the concern as a whole; i.e. the functionaries tend to pursue the technical improvement of means, rather than the accomplishment of the ends of the concern;
(c) the reconciliation, for each level in the hierarchy, of these distinct performances by the immediate superiors, who are also, in turn, responsible for seeing that each is relevant in his own special part of the main task.
(d) the precise definition of rights and obligations and technical methods attached to each functional role;
(e) the translation of rights and obligations and methods into the responsibilities of a functional position;
(f) hierarchic structure of control, authority, and communication;
(g) a reinforcement of the hierarchic structure by the location of knowledge of actualities exclusively at the top of the hierarchy, where the final reconciliation of distinct tasks and assessment of relevance is made;
(h) a tendency for interaction between members of the concern to be vertical, i.e. between superior and subordinate;
(i) a tendency for operations and working behaviour to be governed by the instructions and decisions issued by superiors;
(j) insistence on loyalty to the concern and obedience to superiors as a condition of membership;
(k) a greater importance and prestige attaching to internal (local) than to general (cosmopolitan) knowledge, experience, and skill.

These points constitute the essence of the classical theory of management.

The human relations theory

'Leading groups' is the key phrase in the human relations approach. By 'group' is meant a comparatively small number of people who are gathered together on the basis of their common interests; the term 'face-to-face' indicates the extent of a group.

An organization is conceived as a network of personal relationships within and between groups, such relationships being intimate, informal, and very fluid. There can be a multiplicity of groups within a large enterprise; but because of the focus on groups, there is little awareness of its wholeness. The enterprise is really an over-arching frame within which the groups live and operate.

The concentration on groups and on their internal workings restricts the view in other directions; there is no clear relation to the outside world beyond the general reliance on the level of culture and sophistication in the world without which the groups could not function. The dominant personality in this type of organization is the well-educated, mature, and sensitive person.

It is from such people that the real momentum in the organization comes; the initiative is from within people and it finds its expression in the activity of the groups. The leader, who has to be an even more sensitive person, does not have to push or to direct: he is permissive and non-directive. He seeks to create an atmosphere which will induce people to participate and to express their feelings; he helps to draw out of people what is within them; he prepares the way for them to find the fulfilment of their inner desires. The aim is to create a situation which will lead to maximum happiness and personal satisfaction.

This is achieved through the sharing of goals which are conceived in subjective terms: the goals are the emergent purposes of the group. The decision-making process is essentially that of coming to a common mind within a group, a continuous process by which the deepest feelings in people can be made articulate and given expression. The movement towards decision is from within and from below. Because all have participated in the formulation of goals, so all respond in their attainment: the acceptance of the goals by the group leads to participation in their fulfilment. The pattern of communication is from within a person as each makes his contribution; and then there is sharing with other members of the group and between groups. The sensitivity of members to the feelings of others is an important element in the communication process.

There is control to the extent that each member accepts responsibility for the maintenance of the group and the fulfilment of the tasks commonly agreed upon; the standards are subjective and personal. In the democratic expression of this theory, the participants are subject to control by means of their answerability to their constituents.

The systemic theory

The name of this theory is derived from the concept which is basic to it, namely, a 'system'. A system may be described as a complete entity which consists of, but is greater than, the sum of its constituent parts, which parts retain their own identity although they are interdependent. The internal pattern is governed in part by the purpose for which the system exists and in part by the environment in which it lives; it is in a state of continual adaptation to the world around it so that the expression of its purpose is always relevant to environmental changes.

How does one lead a system? Not by direct action and initiative as in the running of a machine, nor simply by nurturing the parts as in the leading of groups. The function of the leader is to clarify the purpose continually and to interpret the changes in the external world in such a way as to enable the whole system to respond to this context, such response springing from (or the compliance being based on) the commitment of all the members of the organization to the fulfilment of its purpose. The leader also has the responsibility of interpreting the internal changes for what they truly are, namely, the consequence of the adaptation of the organization to a changing environment; in other words, he should help the members of the organization to see that any reshaping of their activities has its source in external influences (and not in any whim or directive of the leader).

This task may be described as the 'monitoring' function in the organization. Within the horizons provided through its operation, two other functions are fulfilled: that which is concerned with the performance of the work for which the organization exists, and that which provides the support for this work to be carried out. These two functions are interdependent: the latter is supportive but not subservient; each function has a distinctive responsibility, and each has a dignity of its own; yet the two interact within the context provided through the monitoring function.

Another way of describing this manner of operation is given by Burns and Stalker (1961, pp. 121–2), applying the same categories that they used to portray the classical theory:

> The *organic* form is appropriate to changing conditions, which give rise constantly to fresh problems and unforeseen requirements for action which cannot be broken down or distributed automatically

arising from the functional roles defined within a hierarchic structure. It is characterized by:

(a) the contributive nature of special knowledge and experience to the common task of the concern;
(b) the 'realistic' nature of the individual task, which is seen as set by the total situation of the concern;
(c) the adjustment and continual re-definition of individual tasks through interaction with others;
(d) the shedding of 'responsibility' as a limited field of rights, obligations, and methods (problems may not be posted upwards, downwards, or sideways as being someone else's responsibility);
(e) the spread of commitment to the concern beyond any technical definition;
(f) a network structure of control, authority, and communication; the sanctions which apply to the individual's conduct in his working role derive more from presumed community of interest with the rest of the working organization in the survival and growth of the firm, and less from a contractual relationship between himself and a non-personal corporation, represented for him by an immediate superior;
(g) omniscience no longer imputed to the head of the concern; knowledge about the technical or commercial nature of the here and now task may be located anywhere in the network; this location becoming the *ad hoc* centre of control, authority, and communication;
(h) a lateral rather than a vertical direction of communication through the organization, communication between people of different rank, also, resembling consultation rather than command;
(i) a content of communication which consists of information and advice rather than instructions and decisions;
(j) commitment to the concern's tasks and to the 'technological ethos' of material progress and expansion is more highly valued than loyalty and obedience;
(k) importance and prestige attach to affiliations and expertise valid in the industrial and technical and commercial milieux external to the firm.

The flexibility of such an administrative process renders impossible an appeal to quantitative standards or to common consent as the control process; instead, control is exercised through the awareness by the expert of the purpose of the organization – this awareness is imparted through training and is constantly renewed by the leader's role of clarifying the goals. The activities of the organization are also judged on the grounds of relevance to a rapidly changing world; there is the continual threat of irrelevance or non-survival if there is failure to adapt; but this ultimate standard of reference may never be operative as a control if the professional dedication of the members to the purpose of the organization is the incentive to respond to environmental changes.

RELATIONSHIPS BETWEEN THE THEORIES

Another way of understanding the theories and acquiring a familiarity with them is to consider some of the important relationships that exist between them, sometimes in terms of similarities, sometimes of contrasts.

For instance, the traditional and the charismatic theories are antithetical: the former is based on the acceptance of the *status quo*, the latter on its rejection; one involves static organizational life, the other dynamic; the course of life in the first is predictable, in the other it is random and unpredictable; decision-making is a continuous process in the traditional approach but discrete in the charismatic. Nevertheless, they share the common characteristic that the response of members is not deliberately calculated, though in one it is non-reflective and in the other it is intuitive.

There are marked contrasts between the traditional and the classical – contrasts which illuminate the fundamentally different approaches to ecclesiastical administration in England and America respectively. The differences are virtually those enshrined in the distinction between *Gemeinschaft* and *Gesellschaft* or between the patrimonial and the bureaucratic. The former is based on the natural and familial relationships between people; the latter is couched in terms of contractual and legal connections. One is expressed in terms of an unformulated, non-reflective approach to organizational life; the other depends on highly conscious, rationalized decision-making.

The comparison between the charismatic and the classical has been made famous by Weber, whose phrase for the classical was 'the routinization of charisma'. What is highly spontaneous in the charismatic is routine in the classical; the random is transposed into the orderly and organized; the seemingly haphazard is replaced by the carefully planned. The organization in the former is a somewhat volatile structure to meet the demands of the intuition; in the latter it is an organized machine designed to fulfil a more permanent purpose. Nevertheless, both forms

THE TYPOLOGY

The theory:		
Symbol	A	C
Name	TRADITIONAL	CHARISMATIC
Focus	Maintaining a tradition	Pursuing an intuition
The organization:		
Conception	Historical institution	Spontaneous creation
Purpose of design	Preserving *status quo*	Giving effect to intuition
Source of momentum	Within heritage	Dynamism of intuition
Relation of parts	Coherent; stable	All focused on intuition
Relation to environment	Attuned to, embedded in, static society	Rejection of *status quo*; articulates changes
Decision-making process:		
Main subjects	Recurrent items	Critical issues
Nature & perception of goals	Generally assumed	Highly explicit
Degree of consciousness	Non-reflective	Spontaneous
Discrete or continuous	Continuous; recurrent	Discrete; unpredictable
Mainspring of decision	Announcement of custom	Proclamation of intuition
Communication of decision	Transmission of heritage	Magnetic influence
Nature of response	Implicit consent	Intuitive accord
Leadership:		
Dominant personality	Elders; wise; sacred	Enlightened
Functions of leader	Voice of tradition; source of wisdom; nurturer; guardian	Prophetic; inspirational
Control process:		
Main factors	Strength of tradition; little awareness of alternatives	Judgemental character of intuition; potential withdrawal of adherents

X CLASSICAL Running a machine	Y HUMAN RELATIONS Leading groups	Z SYSTEMIC Adapting a system
Mechanistic structure	Network of relationships	System; living organism
Maximizing efficiency	Maximizing happiness	Maximizing relevance
Leadership drive	Within individuals	In system; external changes
Mechanical linkage	Fluid; informal	Interdependent
Device for managing mass, homogeneous environment	Reflection of cultured, democratic society	Attuned to changing and complex environment
Efficient performance	Group goals	Adaptation to change
Objective; quantitative	Subjective; emergent	Definitive; unifying
Conscious; calculated	Articulation of feelings	Highly conscious
Discrete; rationalized	Continuous; emergent	Continuous
Issue of orders	Consensus in groups	Expert initiative
Detailed directives	Shared	Interpreted by leader
By coercion	Participation	Immediate adaptation
Aggressive; domineering	Sensitive; cultured	Expert; technician
Directive; organizing	Permissive; non-directive; creates right atmosphere; draws out	Interprets environment; clarifies goals; monitors change
Specific standards set by top management	Individual sense of responsibility; answerability to constituents	Conscientiousness of expert; corrective of goals; threat of non-survival

of operation depend very largely on one man whether he is the intuitive leader or the authoritarian director, and sometimes their behaviour can appear very similar.

The classical and human relations theories are contrasted at almost every point; in fact the latter theory was virtually created as a protest against the inhuman character of the former. An epigram, coined by Warren G. Bennis (1959), which expresses the difference between them is that the classical theory is in terms of 'organizations without people' and the human relations theory is about 'people without organization'. The former is impersonal; the latter personal. In the classical theory, the impetus in an organization comes from above; in the human relations theory, it comes from below. One is directive; the other non-directive. One organization is rigid; the other is free. Yet the very contrasts point to a common characteristic of these two approaches to organizational life: they both represent extreme or exaggerated positions. They are in opposition; yet both fail to take into account the twofold necessity of structure and personal concern. Further, it is possible for the attention given to either or both of these considerations to distract from such issues as task and environment.

The relation of the traditional to the systemic is noteworthy, particularly for those who inherit the English background to this field of study. There is a considerable affinity between the two theories: both involve a systemic conception of the organization, although in the traditional view this tends to be obscured by the static character of the body; and both are based on a complete rapport with the environment. The difference lies in that the traditional theory is suited only to an unchanging situation, whereas the systemic is valid for all situations from the unchanging to the highly fluid and complex.

The charismatic theory is related to a highly volatile situation; an intuitive leader can often crystallize the forces of change in a society and create an organization that is adapted to the new situation. This process – which can be random, intuitive, and disruptive of existing organization – is conceived as being conscious, deliberate, and coherent in the systemic theory.

The comparison between the classical and the systemic is particularly relevant to the American scene; but it is also valuable in the English setting in that it shows that there can be a serious approach to organizational life which does not have the much-feared implications of the classical theory. Many of the points of contrast can be noted by placing alongside each other the two statements by Burns and Stalker. These authors investigated a number of business enterprises and noted that they could be ranged along a continuum from the rigid to the flexible – from the extreme position at one end represented by the classical theory to the other pole of the systemic theory. Perhaps the fundamental difference between the two positions can be expressed epigrammatically: in the former, the situation must fit the organization; in the latter, the organization must fit the situation. However, there is a basic similarity in that both theories involve a consciously unified structure, but for fundamentally different reasons: in the classical theory, it is for the sake of centralization, efficiency, and rigid control; in the systemic theory, on the other hand, it is for the sake of expressing the unity of the organization and the commitment of all its members to its one common purpose so that the whole body might respond to changing situations.

Both the human relations and systemic theories depend on a full and free response by the members of the organization; in the former, however, the arrangement is so fluid as to be amorphous and unstructured, whereas there is a clear form of organization in the latter though it is highly flexible. Moreover, the response in the systemic is related to clearly perceived purposes and to the external world; whereas the kind of participation envisaged in the human relations theory need have no relation to these factors.

FURTHER POINTS OF REFERENCE

A further way of understanding the theories and the relationships between them is to consider lines of information across the chart according to a chosen topic of reference.

Thus the question of how conflict is dealt with is illuminating. In the traditional theory, an undisturbed pattern of life is envisaged; but there may be forces which impinge on the organization and threaten its stability. The characteristic reaction is to turn away from such forces, reject them, ignore them.

On the other hand, a charismatic type of leader thrives on conflict; challenges are welcomed, and the overcoming of contrary forces is the very life-blood of this method of operating.

Typical of the classical theory is the way of domination. Forces of opposition, virtually built into this type of organization in which are stressed the contrary interests of the leader and the led, are dealt with by coercion and brought into subjection to the directives of the authoritative leader.

As regards the human relations theory, the common way of tackling conflict is to try to reach some compromise so that all parties can be satisfied.

A term used to describe the method of handling conflict in accordance with the systemic theory is 'integration'. The idea is to see the creative element in the force which is manifest in a conflicting form and to allow its positive contribution to be made in such a way that the organization is enriched by it.

In this way, instructive comparisons can be made between the several theories, and the points of comparison thus spelled out help to build up a fuller picture of the respective syndromes.

CHAPTER 4

The Theory in Theological Terms

In the preceding chapter, an outline was given of the various theories of organization that underlie all administrative studies including ecclesiastical administration. The several approaches may be compared and judged on managerial grounds, and such a critique would have a general validity in the various fields of study. But in ecclesiastical administration, there are standards of judgement beyond the organizational level because this branch of administrative study is concerned with organizations whose character is ultimately defined in theological terms. The organizations are churches or religious bodies whose foundations can be expressed in terms of Christian doctrine. The evaluation of ecclesiastical administration must then take account of this distinctive feature. Hence the final standard of reference in considering the various theories of organization is whether they are consonant with or inimical to the theological character of ecclesiastical bodies.

The first step in the theological critique is to consider some obvious points of correlation between organizational theory and statements of doctrine. In each theory there is the major topic of the conception of the organization: where the organization is theological in character, the issue becomes the doctrine of the church. Another organizational feature is the relation of the enterprise to its environment: is not the counterpart of this the doctrine of church and society? The nature of leadership in an organization is also important; and so the functions of the leader become the roles of the minister in the church – in general terms, the doctrine of the ministry. Further, what is said about the goals of an organization can readily be transposed into a consideration of the purpose of the church.

Beyond these overt relationships between organizational theory and theology, there are a number of issues which are basic presuppositions. The nature of compliance in an organization involves some fundamental assumptions about human nature which are essentially theological. Implicit also are questions about the nature of God and of man's salvation. These issues are explored up to the point of seeing that the relationship of organizational theory and theology is not merely a chance correlation on a few selected topics but rather the expression of similar ways of thinking about life itself. The two disciplines are rooted in a common stock of ideas. The classical theory of management is the organizational expression of the mechanistic outlook; and such an outlook has shaped theological thinking in a number of significant areas. The traditional approach has its expression in both managerial and doctrinal fields; likewise the systemic theory and some important Christian doctrines share the common conception of a system.

The purpose of this chapter, then, is to show this fundamental relationship between the organizational and the theological, noting which theory or theories have roots in the Bible and which are central to, or opposed to, the mainstream of Christian thinking. In this way, the ultimate critique of ecclesiastical administration will be established having regard to the theological factor that distinguishes this branch of administrative study from its counterparts in other kinds of organization.

THE DOCTRINE OF THE CHURCH

The theological conceptions of the church corresponding to the several theories can be considered by reference to one major theological work, Paul S. Minear's *Images of the Church in the New Testament* (1960) – a book having a number of features that make it appropriate for this particular exercise.

The author, though a Congregational minister, did not express a narrow denominational viewpoint; he wrote the work in the œcumenical context of the Faith and Order studies of the World Council of Churches. The focus is on the New Testament, and Minear gave what is claimed to be the most comprehensive treatment of all the images therein, some ninety-six in all. There may be some argument about his interpretations but not about the completeness of his work.

The main advantage of the study for the present purpose is that the author came to grips with the modern idiom in such a way as to render the thought forms of his theology amenable to transposition without unnecessary linguistic barriers. His continual awareness of the sociological and historical dimensions of the nature of the church meant that his study was couched in terms very similar to those of organizational theory.

After expounding a series of some thirty images which he classed as 'minor', Minear went on to the four major pictures which encompass the remainder of the New Testament terms. These are the images of 'the people of God', 'the new creation', 'the fellowship in faith', and 'the body of Christ'.

In his exposition of the four images, the author drew attention to the main emphasis that each contributes to the doctrine of the church. In the image of 'the people of God' the historical dimension is stressed; the cosmic element appears in the idea of 'the new creation'; the personal factor is uppermost in the conception of 'the fellowship in faith'; and 'the body of Christ' image is based on the corporate quality.

The value of such distinguishing features is that they suggest an immediate correlation with the definitive terms of organizational typology. The historical element is important in the traditional position; the cosmic qualities are inherent in the charismatic approach; the personal element determines the character of the human relations outlook; and the corporate emphasis points to the systemic theory. This is a hopeful beginning to the transposition.

The classical theory

There is one significant omission: there is no point of correlation with the classical theory. Even among the minor images, there do not seem to be any that fit; the only images that could conceivably be stretched to a classical model are those to do with constructions such as 'God's building'. The conclusion is that a church conceived on classical lines has no foundation in the New Testament: there is nothing to give validity to such points as rationalization, the mechanistic structure and relationships, the discrete parts joined in a mechanical way. The handling of ecclesiastical situations in a way that implies these elements is contrary to the New Testament position; church organization on classical lines has no basis in biblical doctrine – but it has a theology, namely, that there are whole areas of life and activity in the church that are separate from God and organized regardless of the biblical nature of the church.

Another way in which classical principles have appeared in the church has been by attributing to a divine source the nature of the church's structure. The structure of the Roman Catholic Church has been understood in this way: there is the typical organizational pyramid with the pope at the apex and the hierarchies ranged below on ever-widening levels. This organization is believed to derive not from human initiative but from a divine source and sanction. That is, a theological foundation is provided for a church organized on classical lines; but the question remains whether this foundation is adequate and whether the classical model is appropriate – the extremes of ultramontanism, the mechanistic view of infallibility and of the exercise of authority, the 'pipe-line' theory of apostolic succession, are grounds for doubt. The new currents of thought in the papacies of John XXIII and his successor and in the second Vatican Council may be evidence of the reshaping of the structure (and perhaps also the doctrine) of the church on lines other than the classical theory of organization.

The human relations theory

One of the main biblical pictures of the church is 'the fellowship in faith'. Minear included in this group such images as: the common life of the sanctified, the faithful, disciples, followers, the witnessing community, friends, the brotherhood. All these share an emphasis on fellowship and personal relationships.

The expectation was thus aroused in Minear's mind, as it may also be in the minds of many others, that these images are the theological counterpart of the kind of organization envisaged in the human relations theory – an organization that is a network of personal relationships, made up of groups of people who share common interests, and depending on the intimacy of human association and accord.

However, when Minear explored the various images, his expectation was confounded: the images are couched in an entirely different language from that which is used in the human relations theory, and their presuppositions are entirely different. The images are about a relationship with God; the church is constituted by Him, not by human initiative or association; and the aspect of personal relationships, though present, is incidental to and derived from the fundamental divine orientation. Thus the church, though described in images which appear to correspond to the terms of the human relations theory, is essentially a divinely constituted and not a human society. Nevertheless, the divine society does have a human manifestation; there are personal relationships within the church; and these relationships, though not constitutive of the church, can be governed by the general principles of Christianity derived from the teaching and example of Christ.

Minear summed up the argument in these words (pp. 161–2):

> In planning this chapter of our study, we expected to survey those images which would throw the greatest light upon the intrachurch dimensions and upon the distinctive quality of its human relations. Actually this kind of division has proved to be impossible. The images draw their basic meaning from the central relationship to the work of Father, Son, and Spirit, and not from their immediate social components. Actually, none of them is drawn directly from the stock of analogies by which the cohesion of social groupings is normally indicated. What do the analogies, whether of saints, of disciples, of the Way, of slaves, say intrinsically about the interstices of community life [the personal relationships in an organization]? Almost nothing in themselves. It was only by the application of these analogies to the field of human relations that their social values became apparent. This application of the images was determined neither by the mental picture conjured up by the words nor by adeptness in rhetorical juggling, but by the total tradition of the message and mission of Jesus Christ.

In other words, personal relations may be shaped by theological standards, but it does not follow that the human relations theory is necessarily based in biblical theology or that the kind of organization envisaged in the theory is divinely founded. On the contrary, this kind of organization is a voluntary, human creation; and this is a denial of the doctrine of the church as a divine society, which is implicit even in those images that appear to provide the theological basis for the human relations approach. The only point of contact that the theory has with the doctrine of the church is that the relationships within a human organization *may* be governed by standards derived from Christian teaching.

Part of the content of 'the fellowship in faith' image can be transferred to the systemic conception of the church; Minear showed how the idea of mutuality, expressed prepositionally in such terms as 'in Christ' and 'with Christ', enriches the meaning of the 'body' image and protects that image from the limitations of 'an anatomical, biological, or sociological figure of speech' (p. 246). Another aspect of the 'fellowship' image has an affinity with the type of organization that is gathered around a charismatic figure: the church, in this view, is the community of those who have responded in faith to the revelation given through the leader. Many of the images grouped in the chapter on 'the fellowship in faith' – the justified, disciples, followers, sons of God – belong to the charismatic pattern.

The charismatic theory

There is a fuller version of the charismatic type of organization expressed in the image of 'the new creation'. The cosmic dimension is uppermost. The old order is overthown; the new order, the kingdom of God, enters in. The process is cataclysmic; there is a great disruption in the course of history; there is a divine breakthrough. The new community is brought into being as the new order supersedes the old.

Some of the minor images also add to the New Testament background of the charismatic view of the church. The first that Minear mentioned in his long list is the image of 'the salt', and he indicated that the more seriously this image is taken, the more it threatens the complacency of the group referred to; there is also the picture of 'the new wine' which bursts the old wineskins; the metaphors of the orchard such as 'the fig tree' and 'the grapevine' have a radical element in that there will be an uprooting of every plant that has not been planted by God.

The charismatic conception of the church is deeply embedded in many parts of the New Testament, but it can lead to false conclusions when taken in isolation from other images in such a way as to exaggerate the radical nature of the change. One corrective of this tendency is the abiding historical emphasis implicit in the image of 'the people of God'.

The traditional theory

The image of 'the people of God' shows how the church belongs to history. Minear said of this aspect (p. 67): 'The basic function in this case is to relate the contemporary Christian generation to that historic community whose origin stemmed from God's covenant promises and whose pilgrimage had been sustained by God's call.' This quotation is almost sufficient in itself to show the kinship between this image and the traditional theory in which is envisaged an organization with an historic continuity through the ages. The point is reinforced by the particular items that come within the scope of the wider image. Some come from political and national analogies: Israel, a holy nation, the twelve tribes, the patriarchs, Abraham's sons, the remnant. Others stress the relationship of the shepherd and his flock, thus using metaphors from an age-old pastoral economy. Priestly and cultic elements are important in such terms as 'the holy city', 'the holy temple', 'the priesthood'; the festivals of the temple calendar, such as 'the passover', are given Christian meaning as the heritage of the past finds its fulfilment in the new society. Minear said of them all (p. 70): 'The galaxy of images that oscillate around this conception [the people of God] served in a distinctive way to place the New Testament church in the setting of the long story of God's dealings with his chosen people.' In this major image, the traditional approach is fully set forth.

In its basic perspective, there is a sound theological foundation for this point of view; but there is an inherent tendency in the traditional theory towards deflection from the original intention and vision: the people of God can become the people of tradition. This was the plight of the church in Old Testament times, and the dynamic intervention by Christ was needed to reassert that the church is the people of God; reformations have taken place since then to restore the true doctrine of the church.

In spite of the weakening of the conception in the traditional view, there is a further worthy element that is important. Next to the focus on historic continuity in the traditional idea of an organization is the awareness of its coherence, of the interdependence of its parts – features which are often obscured by the static condition of the organization. The theological equivalent to this conception is the image of 'the body of Christ'; however, the appropriateness of the image is more clearly seen by studying the systemic theory, in which the relation of the parts within the whole is emphasized much more.

The systemic theory

Of the minor images, some have a clear affinity with the systemic theory, notably that of 'the vine and the branches'; in addition, all the analogies of plant life and growth – the vineyard, the fig tree, the olive tree, God's planting – are consonant with the organic content of the theory.

The most substantial basis in scripture, however, is the image of 'the body of Christ', rated by Minear as the most comprehensive and adequate conception of all.

By drawing on references in I Corinthians 12–14 and Romans 12, Minear stressed the significance of the diversities of ministries in one body and of the relationship between members. He stated (pp. 194–5): 'Each person is not only a member of the one body in Christ; he is also, within the same body, a member of all the other Christians and all of them are members of him. Paul wanted to stress the interdependence of the members.' He went on to discuss the idea of the spiritual body as expounded by St Paul in I Corinthians 15 and showed that the essence of Christian renewal is participation in the death and resurrection of Christ; and such a process of renewal is definitive of the life of the church as well as of all its members. Similar points appear in Colossians, where the images are: 'the head of the church' – the head being the creative source, the first principle, from which the body draws its life; 'the body of this head', in which new life is found through participation in the death of Christ; 'the unity of Jews and Gentiles', of which Minear said (p. 211), 'A new society had appeared that transformed the criteria of social judgement, the bases of social cohesion, and the structures of social institutions'; and 'the growth of the body', which takes place through dying and rising again.

This treatment led to the climax of the New Testament conception of 'the body of Christ' in Ephesians, in which the historical image of 'the people of God' is transposed into the 'body' image; the cosmic dimensions surround the idea; and the character of intrachurch relationships is expressed in terms of the same image:

> And he gave some to be apostles; and some, prophets; and some, evangelists; and some, pastors and teachers; for the perfecting of the saints, unto the work of ministering, unto the building up of the body of Christ: till we all attain unto the unity of faith, and of the knowledge of the Son of God, unto a full grown man, unto the measure of the stature of the fulness of Christ (Ephesians 4 : 11–13).

The completeness of this picture did not blind Minear to the limitations of the conception. He recognized that, on its own, the image of 'the body' could lead to the 'unitarianism of the Son' (meaning that the Son is considered to be the sole divine being); in the study of the interrelation of the images, he showed how the idea of 'the people of God' added an historical dimension to the 'body' image and how the prepositions in the phrases 'with Christ' and 'in Christ', taken from the 'fellowship' image, enriched the conception of mutual relationships in the body. He also wrestled with the objection that the image lacks a cosmic and purposive element, that the conception is inward-looking and cannot be the mainspring for mission. He refuted the statement by reference to the gift of apostleship, which is one member of the body, and to the sharing of suffering consequent upon the conduct of this mission.

He supported this claim by arguing in a way that has a direct reference to organizational theory. He spoke (p. 241) of the common notion of the church as a body of people 'within an organization that has very tangible boundaries', to whom the term 'the body of Christ' is applied 'as a way of saying something additional about this body of people'. However, the biblical conception begins with the cosmic dimensions of the body in which the purposive element was manifest in the incarnation, the conquering element shown forth in the cross, and the effects felt through the ministry of the risen Christ in His body the church. This idea of the church avoids the implications present in the popular view that the church is only a human institution which is confined within limited organizational boundaries, has no necessary relationship with the world around it, and grows by numerical addition. The body of Christ is not restricted by boundaries conceived by man; the essence of its existence and purpose is that it is continually crossing such boundaries as it seeks to encompass all life within the redemptive influence of Christ. This enlargement does not take place merely through an increase in the size of the body but through the growth of the body from within, until the consummation of the divine purpose.

Minear put the argument in these words (p. 243):

> If a boundary exists between the church and the world, it is located and marked by the cross, viewed from one side as God's victory and from the other as scandalous and foolish. But as a boundary the cross is also a bridge for constant two-way traffic. Whatever the distance between church and world, this distance must and can be crossed by the church because it has already been crossed by its head. In the church may be observed the present proleptic beginning of the end, when God will be all in all. The church is the first fruit of a resurrection whose power will be extended to all. The church now is the body where the head is fusing together the one new Man, a growing process in which *all* will attain 'the stature of the fullness of Christ' (Eph. 4 : 9–13). This process is carried on by Christ not through

external extension, not by adding more and more members to his body, but through the inner transformation of life.

The kind of growth in the body of Christ referred to in this quotation is the same as that which takes place in a system. The way in which the church is related to the world and how it crosses the apparent boundaries between itself and the world are akin to the kind of interaction that occurs between a system and its environment. The purpose of the church, which is so important in the conception of 'the body of Christ', corresponds to the goals that determine the shape of a system. In both the theological and organizational viewpoints, there is a recognition of a motive force within the respective systems. Both are conceived in similar terms of wholes in which there are interdependent parts. Thus, on all major points, there is an affinity between the conception of an organization according to the systemic theory and the doctrine of the church as 'the body of Christ'. The fact that this is the major image of the church in the New Testament means that the notion of a system has a very important theological counterpart.

By contrast, to consider the body of Christ in mechanistic terms, as proposed in the classical theory, is to do a serious injustice to the doctrine; an equally serious failing is to consider the divine body as though it were a merely human society on the lines of the human relations theory. The conceptions of the organization in the traditional and charismatic theories have theological analogues, but they also have inherent limitations. Neither is capable of expressing fully the central biblical doctrine of the church – only the systemic theory can do this.

THE DOCTRINE OF CHURCH AND SOCIETY

Another major factor in determining the patterns of leadership is the relation of the organization to its environment. Where the organization is the church, the issue immediately becomes the relation of the church to society – this is essentially a theological matter. What each theory has to offer on this point can be seen by reference to a particular theological treatise on the subject – Niebuhr's *Christ and Culture* (1951).

This book is perhaps the most searching inquiry into the matter and it deals with an even wider perspective than that envisaged in terms of the relation of the church to society or of the organization to the external world. Nevertheless, the fundamental issue is the same: the church has an intimate relationship with Christ and a statement about one implies something about the other; and the way in which Niebuhr defined 'culture' is very close to what is meant by 'society' or 'environment'.

The book has the advantage of being couched in such language as to preclude many barriers that would otherwise hinder the transposition from theology to organizational theory. Niebuhr, besides being a theologian of note, was a sociologist; and so he was sensitive to the kind of interdisciplinary exercise that is at the basis of the present correlation between the doctrine of church and society and the issue of enterprise and environment.

The charismatic theory

The first position expounded by Niebuhr is that of opposition: 'Christ against culture'. He said (p. 54): 'Whatever may be the customs of the society in which the Christian lives, and whatever the human achievements it conserves, Christ is seen as opposed to them, so that he confronts men with the challenge of an "either-or" decision.' This is essentially the charismatic position – the rejection of the existing society and of the *status quo;* and Niebuhr's treatment of 'The New People and "The World"' (pp. 58–68) has many affinities with the conception of 'the new creation' – in which are expressed the cosmic dimensions of the charismatic doctrine of the church. Further, Niebuhr drew attention to the single-heartedness and sincerity of those who adopt this position, characteristics which also describe the charismatic figure and the loyalty of his followers. He went on to point out the inadequacies of this view and how it is impossible to reject culture completely and still live in this world; if one culture is rejected, another culture is assumed, and this biases the character of the new order, so that its original purity cannot be maintained.

The human relations theory

In the second posture, the opposition is changed to agreement: Christ becomes the fulfilment of the aspirations of culture. What is inherent in society reaches its culmination in the life and teaching of Christ; He is the expression of all that is finest and noblest in man. In terms of church and society, the church is the human institution that is the epitome of man's achievements and cultural aspirations; within the church, man becomes his real self. Niebuhr covered a wide range of historical illustrations of 'the Christ of culture'. The human relations theory, based on the same fundamental approach, is mainly confined to one area of history referred to by Niebuhr when he said (p. 54): 'In our time answers of this kind are given by Christians who note the close relation between Christianity and Western civilization, between Jesus' teachings or the teachings about him and democratic institutions.' Although there is much of virtue and hope in this position, Niebuhr was aware of a serious limitation. His use of the term 'accommodation' in the sense that Christ is accommodated to cultural factors is akin to the charge that the human relations approach ultimately becomes an attitude of acquiescence – accepting the world as it is and dealing only with its consequences.

In the conception of 'the Christ of culture', Niebuhr included an element beyond the scope of the human relations theory; he saw in culture more than the emergent aspirations which found their fulfilment in Christ. He recognized the permanence of the cultural world and of the function of Christ in its continuance (p. 54): 'He confirms what is best in the past, and guides the process of civilization to its proper goal. Moreover, he is a part of culture in the sense that he himself is part of the social heritage that must be transmitted and conserved.' This approximates to the position of the traditional theory in its emphasis on the maintenance of the historical society with its continuing heritage.

The traditional theory

Such a view belongs more, however, to the third of Niebuhr's categories, that of 'Christ above culture', a conception that expresses the traditional position in its finest form. No longer is it a choice of 'either-or'; there is a synthesis of Christ and culture. It is not a matter of divine revelation solely, nor the mere bringing out of what is within man; Christ 'enters into life from above with gifts which human aspiration has not envisioned and which human effort cannot attain unless he relates men to a supernatural society and a new value-centre' (p. 55). True culture enshrines the continuing heritage of human civilization which at every point is enriched by the supernatural dimensions and meaning. Niebuhr recognized that there was much in this view of the central Christian position; but he also saw its inadequacies. What happens in time of change when the culture is threatened? There will be a turning 'to the defence of that temporal foundation for the sake of the superstructure it carries' (p. 151). The synthesists have no guard against the institutionalization of the gospel; the church becomes embedded in society; and the culture becomes the repository of all the supernatural treasures, so much so that in the face of change the attempt is made to preserve the culture, an attempt that is equated with the preservation of the gospel itself.

The classical theory

Niebuhr's fourth posture was the coexistence in paradox of both Christ and culture; this has some elements which indicate its affinity with the position of the classical theory. In the classical point of view, the opposition inherent in the paradox is recognized: the organization and the environment, church and society, Christ and culture, are different entities. Niebuhr, in his conception, envisaged the permanent tension in which a Christian lived as he faced conflicting but unavoidable loyalties. In the classical position, it is recognized that there are conflicting loyalties, but the regard for culture is not unavoidable: there is a way of resolving the tension and that way is by domination. Ultimately the world must fit the church; culture must be dominated by Christ and made to serve His ends. This view is similar to the dualist's view that there cannot be any accommodation of Christ to culture; it is based on a lack of respect for culture itself which is to some extent inherent in the dualist position; but the classical position is free from any obligation towards the values in society. All virtue and truth are on the side of the church; and only by being brought within the dominance of the church, by force if necessary, is there any salvation for the world. This is clearly different from the fourth position of Niebuhr; but it is still a theological position by which the classical theory can be judged. It has had its exponents in the church; it has been given expression in some phases of history; but it cannot be said to represent the standard Christian position because it implies a disrespect for the work of God in creation and culture.

The systemic theory

The fifth of Niebuhr's categories is that of 'Christ the transformer of culture'. In this view, 'Christ is seen as the converter of man in his culture and society, not apart from these, for there is no nature without culture and no turning of man from self and idols to God save in society' (p. 56). Anything that happens by way of transformation in man has its counterpart in the transformation in society – the divine strategy comprehends both. Moreover, the culture, as well as man in it, is the creation of God though it may have been diverted from its true destiny by the sin of man. The remedy is, however, but part of the same divine operation; the conversionist 'seeks to hold together in one movement the various themes of creation and redemption, of incarnation and atonement. . . . The Word that became flesh and dwelt among us, the Son who does the work of the Father in creation, has entered into human culture that has never been without his ordering action' (pp. 194–5). The consummation of the action is the lifting up of all life into the kingdom of God.

The essence of the transforming process is Christ's identification with man in his culture; this is the incarnation; it embraces His 'living with men in great humility, enduring death for their sakes, and rising again from the grave' (p. 193). The very identification becomes the means whereby His purpose is fulfilled.

What is true of Christ is true of His church: its character, its method, and its purpose are defined by reference to Him. The church, the body of Christ, adapts to the world in which it lives; it does not succumb to it or merely acquiesce in it, but adapts in order that its work in society might be accomplished. The method is by way of humble service rather than by revolution or domination. Yet, because the church is itself in the world, it stands in need of transformation, too; and through the renewal of its inner life it brings the revitalizing influence of Christ to the world around it.

In the managerial terms of the relation of the organization to its environment, the position is that of the adaptation of the enterprise to its changing external situation in order that it may fulfil its purpose – and do so in a way that is relevant to its context. At the same time, there is a continual reshaping of the system as the whole body responds to the new conjunction of purpose and situation. These are the terms of the systemic theory; and this theory alone, of all the possible approaches, is capable of rendering in organizational terms the exalted doctrine of Christ and culture, of church and society, which Niebuhr recognized as being the great central position of the Christian faith.

THE DOCTRINE OF THE MINISTRY

The third area of consideration in which the organizational profiles can be immediately transposed into theological terms is that of the functions of the leader; these correspond to the roles of the minister. The conception of leadership becomes the doctrine of the ministry.

The essence of the doctrine of the ministry (Moberly, 1899; Niebuhr, 1956; Robinson, 1960, 1961; Welch, 1936) is that it is the ministry of Christ: it belongs to Him; it is fully expressed in Him; and it is derived from Him. It is the ministry of Christ incarnate, crucified, risen, ascended, glorified.

Within this total ministry, it is possible to distinguish three roles: those of prophet, priest, and pastor. These three roles were exercised in Old Testament times; and they were given their definitive orientation in the New Testament in the light of the ministry of Christ. He is supremely the prophet, the priest, and the pastor. All three elements are important; each is essential to a full understanding of the ministry; the neglect of one means an incomplete ministry. Moreover, there is no conflict between the roles: they are supportive of one another.

The full ministry comprising these three roles is the ministry of Christ; because it is His, so it belongs to His body, the church. Moreover, those who are chosen or ordained to exercise this ministry do so in this context. The ministry does not belong to individuals: it belongs to the body and to Christ. Individual ministers exercise their office by expressing in their lives what is true of the whole church and of Christ Himself.

This is the doctrine of the ministry by which can be judged the theological counterparts of the roles of a leader appropriate to the respective theories.

The first four theories

The function of the leader in terms of the traditional theory is shaped by the dominant concern for maintaining the tradition. The teaching role is important: through teaching, the next generation is brought up in the faith; it is the means whereby the heritage is transmitted. The pastoral function is in the nurturing and encouraging of people, in the fatherly care of the family, and in providing for their spiritual sustenance. The priestly element is in the unfolding of the age-old mysteries that enshrine the sacredness of the tradition; and in the ministering of the sacraments there is the expression in ritual form of the abiding treasures of a divinely governed society. Nevertheless, the prophetic aspect is missing: this has no place, since it would lead to the disturbance of the *status quo*. The absence of this element can lead, as it did in Old Testament times, to the degeneration of the teaching function: the teacher became the scribe who was concerned with the preservation of the tradition in a legalist way. The priest became a cultic and ritualistic figure engrossed in the sacrificial system.

The prophetic role, absent in the traditional theory, is dominant in the charismatic. The prophet is the theological equivalent to a charismatic leader: one who proclaims a compelling message and attracts followers to his cause almost by the very magnetism of his personality. But this is a one-sided kind of ministry, exalting prophecy to the neglect of the priestly and pastoral roles. Even considered on its own, such an approach has limitations in that prophecy cannot be evoked at will; it can be random and haphazard; and this kind of ministry has always been dogged by the almost unanswerable problem of distinguishing between true and false prophets.

The main roles of the minister according to the classical theory are those of organizer and administrator. Of them both it can be said that they are not biblical in character; this is the same judgement that has been made of the classical conception of the church. These roles cannot be identified with or related to the biblical roles of prophet, priest, and pastor; in fact, their character is quite inimical to the New Testament conceptions of the ministry. Therein lies the source of the conflict that arises for a minister should he adopt this theory: these are not the roles for which he was ordained. The increasing preoccupation with them adds to the minister's frustration.

The personal element in the human relations theory means that something of the essential nature of the ministry is restored when a minister follows this pattern. His role in leading groups is pastoral; not in the paternal way as in the traditional theory, but in the sense of being a counsellor. Such a ministry involves a high degree of sophistication and sensitivity; and it requires a knowledge of psychology and psychiatry. This kind of ministry is personal to a point that almost removes it from its theological context in the same way that the human relations conception of an organization is based on human rather than godward relationships. Absent from this picture of the ministry is any reference to the roles of prophet and priest, again because these roles involve theological perspectives. Nevertheless, the human relations idea of the ministry has a dignity when expressed in terms such as 'democratic pastoral leadership'; the minister is envisaged as being in charge of an organization in which fundamental human rights are respected, leadership is exercised through persuasion, and response is sought through intelligent co-operation. However, the dignity is derived from an exalted view of human relations rather than from the divine quality of the office.

The systemic view of prophet, priest, and pastor

What is the doctrine of the ministry that is implied in a systemic pattern of leadership? How can the function of the systemic leader be related to the roles of prophet, priest, and pastor?

The essence of systemic leadership is that the leader has a dual concern with the purpose of the organization and with its environment, both of which he interprets to the organization in such a way that the whole body may respond accordingly. In theological terms, the concerns are the purpose of God (and of His church) and the world in which the church lives; and the church leader's task is to express these concerns in such a way that the church adapts to such a conjunction of purpose and situation. This is the essence of the biblical conception of prophecy – the making known of the will of God in a particular situation. This task, however, does not belong solely to the leader; it is shared with those who have knowledge and understanding of these issues and who have the capacity to communicate to others. The ultimate objective is that the whole church might be truly prophetic in character through its total response to the two definitive elements of its being. This conception of prophecy is much more complete than that envisaged in the charismatic theory. In a world that is changing rapidly and is also very complex, the latter type of prophecy has little relevance. Prophecy cannot be left to one person: the issues are too complex and profound for any one man; moreover, the mere pursuit of intuitions does not do justice to the complexities of the situation or to the intelligence of people. There is a need for expert knowledge on both theological and social questions so that the prophetic voice of the church is presented, not by self-appointed orators, nor necessarily by those in the hierarchy, but by those who have the time and scholarship to explore the concerns of the moment.

Is there any way in which the systemic leader exercises the function of a priest? Not in the sense of being one who deals in ancient mysteries, nor in the individualist sense of being a mediator between a God-up-there and man-down-here; but in the sense of sharing in the priestly work of the body of Christ. The body of Christ is that through which the redemptive work of Christ is carried on in the world, reconciling God and man. The priesthood of the body cannot be understood without reference to the relation of that body to the world, that is, to the doctrine of church and society. The transformation of society and the bringing of all life within the redemptive power of Christ constitute the essential priestly task of the body of Christ and of the ministry within it. In keeping with this is the function of the leader conceived in systemic terms. He is in a position of responsibility within the whole organization and is especially concerned with the relation of that body to its environment. He is at the forefront of the church's task in respect to the world around it; he is on the boundary between the church and its environment; he interprets one to the other. He gives expression to what is taking place in the interplay between the body of Christ and its cultural context whereby the purpose of the church is accomplished in a relevant way. The priestly role is thus intimately associated with the prophetic.

It may appear that the pastoral role of the systemic leader is diminished: he is detached from the kinds of preoccupation that a pastor is involved in according to the traditional or human relations theories. However, the kind of ministry envisaged in these last two theories can be reduced to a concern for individuals as though this were the essence of being a pastor. Admittedly it is an important element – witness the shepherd and the one lost sheep in the flock of a hundred; but the object of the shepherd's care is primarily the flock, not one individual or a collection of individuals. This is recognized in the terms of the traditional theory where the leader is concerned with the nurture of the people of God, not primarily with one or several of God's people. The corporate element is even more explicit in the terms of the systemic theory: the pastoral ministry is exercised in relation to the whole organization of which the theological counterpart is the body of Christ; all that a systemic leader does is in relation to that body. True pastoral care is the ministry of Christ towards His body the church, and through that body to all men.

In these ways, the theology of the ministry corresponding to the systemic theory means a full restoration of the cherished roles of prophet, priest, and pastor in the one complete ministry rooted in biblical thinking and belonging to the whole church and to its head.

The systemic view of bishops, priests, and deacons

Another way of comprehending the systemic picture of the ministry is to consider the theological equivalents of the three necessary functions in an organization as understood in this theory. What has been said above about the ministry applies primarily to the person who exercises the monitoring function. But there are two other functions: that of doing the work for which the organization exists – which in the case of the church may be called the 'ministering' function; and that of providing the necessary support for such work – this may be called the 'maintaining' function. These three functions in a system are the managerial counterparts of the three orders of ministers in the church: bishops, priests, and deacons.

Most of the debate about the ministry has been about its theological foundation; but the threefold ministry may have an organizational rationale as well. This is understandable when it is recognized that the mainstream of thinking about the nature of the church has drawn on the same basic concepts as the systemic theory. The development of the three orders may be related to the awareness of the systemic nature of the church and of the three functions in the organizational shape of a system.

The early history of the ministry tends to support this view (Cross, 1957, s.v. 'bishop', 'presbyter', 'priest', 'deacon'). The interchangeable use of the terms 'bishop' and 'presbyter' in the New Testament is normally in a context which implies the exercise of the monitoring function of oversight (e.g. Acts 20 : 17, 28). Whereas the former title has retained this connotation, the word 'presbyter' came to be reserved for those who performed the ministering function, which function came to be less and less a part of the bishop's work except for certain rites which required episcopal orders. The diaconate was a separate office concerned mainly with material things – for example, the collection and distribution of alms – on the lines of the maintaining function; and an archdeacon was the head deacon in a particular place and virtually the bishop's chief administrative officer.

The correlation between the three orders of the ministry and the three functions in a system clearly seen in the early history of the ministry has become obscured and confused in the course of later developments. Perhaps through the influence of the classical theory, the three orders have come to be regarded as a hierarchy with all three doing the same work of ministering but ranging from the comprehensive to the inferior. Thus a bishop has been regarded as an omnicompetent minister; the priest has become somewhat limited in that he cannot administer the sacraments of confirmation and holy orders; and the deacon has been restricted even further to assisting at the Holy Communion and baptizing only in the absence of the priest. In the Anglican situation, the diaconate has become so inferior that it has become but a year's apprenticeship to the priesthood; and even when a person is made a perpetual deacon, it is only so that he can perform limited ministering functions on a permanent basis. The idea that the diaconate has a purpose and dignity of its own has been virtually lost; and many who in fact do the diaconal work are not ordained at all. Another anomaly is that an archdeacon must first become a priest. A fairly common career pattern is as follows: a man is trained for ministering (this is normally the only kind of training provided) and, after a time of apprenticeship as a deacon, he becomes a priest; should he have a flair for administration, he may become an archdeacon and perhaps perform truly diaconal work (the maintaining function); if he does well at this, he may become a bishop, in which office he operates as a 'super-archdeacon', being involved all the more in the maintaining function. In addition, he spends a great deal of time doing ministering work in the form of confirmations; and perhaps the monitoring role is never properly exercised at all.

In considering the difficulties encountered in the development of ecclesiastical administration, especially in England, note was made of the duality of the pastoral and the administrative and of the attempts to comprehend the two: some thought of their opposition, others saw the administrative as a necessary preliminary to the pastoral, and a third view was to regard them as intertwined and illuminating each other. The basic difficulty was the limitation to the two functions that correspond to the ministering and the maintaining; the solution lies in considering the three functions of a system. In this way, bishops are not left trying to reconcile the demands of two apparently antithetical functions, but have primary responsibility for the monitoring function without being immediately responsible for performing the other two. The other orders of ministry provide the responsible officers appropriate to the ministering and maintaining functions, and each function has a dignity and a responsibility in its own right. Their relationship is shaped according to a common response to the context provided by the monitoring function and according to the supportive position of the maintaining in relation to the ministering function.

Clarity of perception about the functions of the leader in the systemic theory of management can contribute to the understanding of the doctrine of the ministry in such a way as to restore the meaning of the threefold ministry of bishops, priests, and deacons, and also to express the content of the biblical roles of prophet, priest, and pastor. By contrast, the other theories of management have theological analogues in inadequate or unacceptable conceptions of the ministry.

THE PURPOSE OF THE CHURCH

One of the points in the delineation of the theoretical profiles is the nature of the goal of the organization and the way in which it is perceived. The parallel in theological terms is the consideration of the purpose of the church. The correlation does not mean that the purpose of the church can be derived from the study of organizational theory; but the theory is relevant to the way in which the purpose is defined and perceived and to the way in which it is attained or thwarted.

An important study of the theological issue is Niebuhr's *The Purpose of the Church and its Ministry* (1956); again, the author's knowledge of both theology and sociology facilitates the comparative study between the two fields. Although his primary interest in this book was in theological schools, his treatment is relevant to all religious organizations.

He asked (p. 27): 'What are the objectives of the Church?' He noted some of the manifold answers that are given: the nurturing of the Christian life and the salvation of souls; the building up of the life of the church; the preaching of the gospel; the dispensation of the sacraments; the strengthening of the life of prayer and worship; the winning of disciples to the Christian cause; the fulfilling of responsibility in society. The list could be extended indefinitely as each particular body or group or department or society expressed its own distinctive aim. 'The multiplicity of goals corresponds to the pluralism in the Church that is made up of many members, each with its own function' (p. 28); but 'the question is whether there is one end beyond the many objectives as there is one Church in the many churches. Is there one goal to which all other goals are subordinate, not necessarily as means to end, but as proximate objectives that should be sought only in relation to a final purpose?' (p. 28). Is there a 'final unifying consideration that modifies all the special strivings' (p. 29)?

Niebuhr recognized that there were divergent emphases in the attempts to express this ultimate goal: differences between Protestant and Catholic, between Bible-centred and church-centred approaches, between the humanist stress on the Son of Man and the theological stress on the Son of God. Yet commitment in terms of one or other of these possible attitudes is somewhat less than the 'great central position of the historic Church' for 'nothing less than God – albeit God in the mystery of his being as Father, Son and Holy Spirit – is the object towards which Scriptures, Church and Jesus Christ himself direct those who begin by loving them' (p. 31).

He went on (p. 31): 'Is not the result of all these debates and the content of the confessions or commandments of all these authorities this: that no substitute can be found for the definition of the goal of the Church as the *increase among men of the love of God and neighbor*?' Alternative phrases may be used – 'extending the kingdom of God', 'the reconciliation of God and man' – but the same ultimate objective remains; and in the light of this, 'may it not be that many of our confusions and conflicts in churches and seminaries are due to failure to keep this goal in view while we are busy in the pursuit of proximate ends that are indeed important, but which set us at cross-purposes when followed without adequate reference to the final good?' (pp. 31–2).

If this is the most adequate way of conceiving and expressing in theological terms the purpose of the church, then it is the standard of reference by which the attitudes about goals in the respective theories can be judged.

Such a purpose outlined by Niebuhr may be expressed in catechetical form, as envisaged in the traditional theory; but such statements can be remote from the non-reflective behaviour of members in the organization. Moreover, the pursuit of proximate ends by each part and the consequent complexity in the shape of the structure, which are typical features of this theory in operation, can lead to the obscuring of the professed objective.

The conception of the goal in Niebuhr's terms would be too general for a charismatic type of leader; he would want something more specific around which to rally his followers. The pursuit of such objectives would probably not allow the total objective to be perceived at all.

The emphasis in the classical theory is upon proximate goals expressed in precise quantitative terms; and such an emphasis may preclude a wider vision of the ultimate purpose and would reduce the purpose of the church to numerical and unbiblical terms.

In the human relations approach, the perception of the ultimate goal may never be attained because there is a stress on what emerges from within; there may be a reaching out towards a goal but clarity may not necessarily result from this process.

However, there is a similarity between Niebuhr's conception and that envisaged in the systemic theory. In the systemic approach, there is a clear focus on the ultimate objective, and the focus is maintained by virtue of the inclusion within the structure of the monitoring agent which guides the whole organization in relation to that purpose. Thus the organization is oriented towards the fulfilment of the ultimate objective and there is a built-in corrective to guard against deflection in the direction of the more proximate goals.

In this fourth area of doctrine, as in the other three, it is the systemic theory, when rendered in theological terms, that approximates most closely to the central Christian position.

THE DOCTRINE OF GOD

In the foregoing sections, the main determinants of the organizational profiles have been directly transposed into their theological equivalents; but there can be a further stage beyond these more obvious associations. These doctrinal statements are not isolated positions, but are parts of a whole range of related theological ideas. The further doctrinal propositions can be reached by inquiring into assumptions that are more or less hidden. To uncover these, the process of inference is used in relation to the five theories in the same way that Van Vleck (1937) sought to reveal the theological bases of the patterns of behaviour that he studied. Niebuhr (1951) also developed this kind of inquiry and looked into the deeper implications of the several postures that he analysed in the relation of Christ and culture. Minear (1960) likewise drew attention to other areas of doctrine that had a close association with the respective images of the church.

The traditional view

In connection with the underlying doctrine of God, Minear noted (p. 223) that the image of the people of God, characteristic of the traditional approach, 'appears to stress the work of the Father', and this is supported by reflection on the general nature of that theory. God is the God of history; He was the creator and is now the sustainer and the preserver of that created order, although the element of creativeness is no longer stressed. He created man and called him to his historical pilgrimage; in that journey, God is the beneficent provider, the succourer, the deliverer, watching over His people with fatherly care. He is the source of life and of the wisdom that guides man to his destiny. He sanctifies the sacred events of history and the hallowed places of geography; all phases of human life are blessed by Him.

The major focus is on the initiative of the Father; the Son is of lesser importance. His activity is within the context of the Father's work; His coming into the world did not start anything new – the people of God continued from Old Testament times into the New Testament age without any break in the tradition. The Son corrected the customs of the day but did not fundamentally change the tradition; He Himself was the perfect embodiment of it. He widened its range by the opening of the church beyond Judaism but only in order that all people, as intended in the Abrahamic covenant, might be the sons of Abraham.

In the traditional position, the Spirit has even less place; He is the means whereby the things of tradition are sanctified. He is subservient to the purposes of the Father; He does not have equal status or independent initiative.

The charismatic theory

By contrast, the Spirit is dominant in the charismatic pattern: the Spirit is the irruptive, dynamic, magnetic, and compelling power as on the day of Pentecost. He is not bound by the accepted ways of tradition or the expected patterns of activity. He overthrows the existing order; He breaks forth unpredictably; people are won to His allegiance by the attractive power of His witness and they experience that power within the company of believers. The Son becomes the supreme instance of charismatic leadership to the neglect of the traditional view of His work and of His historical links with the past and with the God of history. The realm of the Spirit stands in contrast with the created order; the Spirit is opposed to all existing society, and so there is a real division between the Spirit and the God who is the author and preserver of creation.

The classical position

There is also a disparagement of the Father in the classical position: the creation is the work of an inferior God, and it is only by the work of man that it is put on its right course. Man is the god in this approach – man with his order and rationality from which springs all that is worthy and valuable in life. Man is the source of overall plans, and everything has to fit into his pattern, even God Himself, whether Father or Son or Spirit. This position represents the essence of the doctrine of original sin, alleviated, perhaps, by some recognition that there is somewhere a source of man's reason. However unpalatable this view may be, there is no better answer when the classical organization in a church is attributed, not to man's rationality, but to God Himself. God is then conceived of as being completely transcendent, the impersonal arbiter of man's fate, a coercive and punitive power, without mercy and without human concern.

The human relations approach

In the human relations view, God is immanent, present in people: the Spirit who stirs within them; the Son who is the embodiment of the finest in their imagination; the Father who is the ultimate source and ground of all goodness, truth, and beauty. God, whether Father or Son or Spirit, is the appellation given to what is basically human; it is the name that expresses the profoundest and most precious feelings in man – a view that is man-centred but much more attractive than the ultimate position of the classical approach.

The systemic position

The element of divine initiative and activity is restored in the systemic position; the assumptions about God are God-centred. God is a God of action; and what the systemic leader does can be only in relation to that action and to that through which the action is accomplished – the body of Christ. The full areas of divine action in creation, redemption, and sanctification are restored; but not in a way that suggests that there are three sequential phases associated individually with the three members of the Trinity. God is one and His purpose one. The Father, Son, and Spirit have been from everlasting; and in unity they all have shared in the single action of divine outreach in a way that does not divide them or the respective areas of action. The posture outlined by Niebuhr as 'Christ the transformer of culture' gives a glimpse of this point (1951, p. 194): 'For the conversionist, however, the creative activity of God and of Christ-in-God is a major theme, neither overpowered by nor overpowering the idea of atonement.'

Niebuhr went on to show that the problem of culture is that of its conversion, not of its replacement. There is no hiatus in the activity of God nor opposition between the persons. He also showed (p. 225) how F. D. Maurice saw 'the universal and present divine possibility of the conversion of mankind from self-centredness to Christ-centredness'; in a similar way, the same possibility is provided in the systemic theory when transposed into theological terms. Ecclesiastical administration is thus saved from the man-centred doctrines of God, whether held in the extreme forms of grim perverseness or optimistic idealism, and from the God-centred doctrines in which there is a tendency to exaggerate the significance of either the Father or the Spirit.

THE DOCTRINE OF MAN

The classical theory

The issue of the doctrine of man implicit in theories of management was raised by McGregor (1960) when he commended the human relations approach in preference to the classical. The classical theory had been silent on this point, but McGregor, by the process of inference, drew out what the theory implied about the nature of man; there were three points (pp. 33–4, italicized sentences only):

1. The average human being has an inherent dislike of work and will avoid it if he can.
2. Because of this human characteristic of dislike of work, most people must be coerced, controlled, directed, threatened with punishment to get them to put forth adequate effort toward the achievement of organizational objectives.
3. The average human being prefers to be directed, wishes to avoid responsibility, has relatively little ambition, wants security above all.

These observations were not couched in theological terms but they were statements about the nature of man which can be transposed into the doctrine of original sin. This estimate of the nature of man tends towards the position of depravity the more the classical theory is pursued; and this is an extreme and not the central position in the Christian doctrine of man.

The human relations view

McGregor presented the other side of the picture when he set forth the assumptions about human nature in the alternative theory (pp. 47–8, italicized sentences only):

1. The expenditure of physical and mental effort in work is as natural as play or rest.
2. External control and the threat of punishment are not the only means for bringing about effort toward organizational objectives. Man will exercise self-direction and self-control in the service of objectives to which he is committed.
3. Commitment to objectives is a function of rewards associated with their achievement.
4. The average human being learns, under proper conditions, not only to accept but to seek responsibility.
5. The capacity to exercise a relatively high degree of imagination, ingenuity, and creativity in the solution of organizational problems is widely, not narrowly, distributed in the population.
6. Under the conditions of modern industrial life, the intellectual potentialities of the average human being are only partially utilized.

In theological terms, this is a modest statement of the doctrine of original righteousness; the extreme position of the human relations approach tends towards the doctrine of the perfectibility of man by his own efforts – a position that is well removed from the central Christian conception of man.

The traditional conception

The traditional position includes a recognition of the magnificent order sustained and preserved by God; and within that divine providence man attains through Christ to his destiny. This position is capable of a profound doctrine of man that is close to the mainstream of Christian thinking; such doctrines are set forth in catechetical form, but the operative view is somewhat different. The security that man feels within the traditional approach can dull his creative and imaginative faculties; no great initiative is expected of him, and he becomes content with such a state. Instead of a doctrine of the fall of man and the redemption through Christ, man is taken to be somewhat innocuous and mildly virtuous, qualities which will make him content with his lot and amenable to the continuance of the *status quo.*

The charismatic theory

In the charismatic view, the issue of the nature of man is sharpened: it is seen in terms of black and white – sinfulness and perfection. Man is rescued by divine intervention from the utter hopelessness of a state of sin into a realm of purity and perfection. The extremes of this position may arouse suspicions as to its adequacy; there can also be assumptions that sin is in the culture and that the way out is to cut oneself off from the world, whereas sin in fact is prevalent and deeply rooted in man himself. Man cannot escape from himself; he can be saved from himself only by the action of God in Christ.

The systemic answer

This is the answer in the systemic position: man moves from being self-centred to being Christ-centred by the divine action; he is saved from himself by being lost in Christ and in the life of the body of Christ. Within that body he shares the death and resurrection of Christ and is caught up into the divine purpose for which that body exists. He finds his true dignity restored, as a creature of God made in His image; an important part of that image is that he shares the creative character of God Himself; he has initiative and responsibility which are saved from being man-centred by virtue of the fact that his whole being is within the body of Christ and within the whole divine outreach in creation, redemption, and sanctification. This conception thus obviates the extreme positions about human nature implicit in the classical and human relations models and it provides for a more adequate remedy for the sin of man than do the other two theories.

FURTHER AREAS OF DOCTRINE

Thus far two main areas of doctrine – God and man – have been considered in showing the assumptions that lie behind the various perspectives on leadership. The procedure can be extended to other issues. In the exposition of the doctrine of man, there was on each point some reference to the doctrine of salvation. Thus, in the traditional posture, there was an inadequate emphasis on the saving work of Christ; in the charismatic approach, the dramatic extent of the change was exaggerated. One part of the classical thinking had affinities with the views of divine action inherent in the doctrines of predestination; the human relations approach – in which is stressed man's ability to attain salvation – is akin to the Pelagian position.

The more this process is continued, the further the issues are removed from being clear assumptions behind the various theories of management to being areas of doctrine which are expressed in similar ways of thinking. Instead of being implicit statements, they tend to be parallel points of view. The method is thus changed from the drawing out of inferences to the use of the typology in existing fields of doctrine. As it has been shown that there are distinct doctrinal positions implicit in the various theories, so the theories can be of some value in understanding and analysing doctrinal positions in which there is a wide divergence of views.

In the field of Christology, the Nestorian view, with its emphasis on the human nature of Christ, represents the kind of thinking that characterizes the human relations approach. The opposing Monophysite view, associated with Eutyches, meant the elimination of the human element in Christ, so much so that He was presented as a divine being who acted in an impersonal, if not mechanistic, way. In the decision of the Council of Chalcedon in 451, both these ways of thinking were rejected as inadequate for the description of the relation of the divine and human natures in Christ.

The impersonal or mechanistic element can also be seen in other areas of theology. Sacramental doctrine has been affected by it; at times the sacraments have been looked upon as almost mechanical means of bestowing divine grace, a view that is expressed in the term *ex opere operato*. By contrast, there is the view in which the human element is emphasized: conscious response and faith are necessary to the point of being the definitive elements in the extreme position known as receptionism. Adequate sacramental theology must take account of the fact that a person is in Christ, a member of His body, and that one does not approach, for example, the sacraments of communion or penance as an outsider who comes to God by the strength of his own faith or by the mere performance of the sacramental rite. The charismatic view of sacraments is that they are superfluous; in that view, divine grace comes directly through revelation and not through what would be regarded as human institutions. Another point of view is to regard the sacraments as traditional rituals of great sacredness marking the main stages in the life of an individual or the events of the historic community.

THEOLOGICAL CONCLUSION

To proceed further in this way would turn this inquiry into a purely theological exercise; but sufficient has been said to show that at all stages – the more obvious transpositions, the hidden assumptions, and the parallel ways of thinking – there is a high degree of affinity between organizational theory and theological doctrines. The two disciplines embody common perspectives: basic approaches to life are expressed on the one hand in theories of management and on the other hand in schools of doctrine.

This study enables theories of management to be judged in theological terms and so have their appropriateness for churches determined in the light of the distinctive character of such bodies. The inquiry has shown that the systemic way of thinking has the greatest weight of biblical support and is nearest to the central stream of Christian thinking; and so the systemic theory of management is supremely suitable for use in the church. The alternative theories are less appropriate, though the traditional and charismatic have some roots in biblical thinking; and the human relations theory is capable at least of expressing Christian principles; but the classical theory is generally inimical to the Christian faith.

Having thus singled out the systemic theory as most appropriate for the study of ecclesiastical administration, it may seem that all that remains to be done is to draw out its implications in detail. Nevertheless, the other theories cannot be set aside completely. One reason is that these theories appear to have a considerable influence in religious bodies, and evidence will be given of how church life has been shaped accordingly. Another reason is that the detailed features of the systemic way of management can be seen all the more clearly by comparison with their counterparts in the alternative theories. Therefore, on most topics, the fivefold typological treatment will be continued, though the preference will always be for the systemic theory because of its theological basis outlined in the present chapter.

PART THREE

The Practice of Ecclesiastical Administration

CHAPTER 5

The General Character of Church Life

The purpose of this chapter is to provide some illustrations of the theory of ecclesiastical administration that has been set forth in the preceding part. The examples show that the general character of church life and of the administrative behaviour of clergy is closely related to one or other of the several approaches outlined in the theoretical discussion.

The illustrations are taken from biographies, from historical treatises, and from case-studies; they include examples from North America and from England; and they range from the national to the local level. Some of the evidence is used again in later discussions of particular administrative topics (hence the reference numbers: A1, A2, .., C1, C2, .., X1, and so on), and at that stage further illustrative material is introduced; but the aim of the presentation at this point is to show what it is like to think and operate in the traditional or the various other ways.

ILLUSTRATIONS OF THE TRADITIONAL THEORY

A1. Up to the very outbreak of the conflict [1914], from the point of view of the ordinary man, Randall Davidson was still rather an increasingly important figure in the background than a great public character: a very cautious and a very wary man, not too anxious to commit himself. With the growing gravity of the War, he gradually emerged. His steadfastness and his devotion to the work in hand made their impression. His refusal to be carried away, whether in ultra-nationalism or ultra-pacifism, begot a confidence in his judgement. There was something massive about him, massive and true. And throughout the four and a half years of the War, on the repeated solemn occasions on which he had to address the whole people at or through special national services, he spoke the brave, strong, and heartening words of a Christian bishop. He said nothing common, or mean – nothing vindictive. On the contrary, he did not hesitate, in the very midst of the conflict, to utter his protests against actions and speeches which seemed to him unworthy of the traditions of his country. It is true that he lacked the high and imaginative ardour of a seer, and set small store by sentimental oratory, or idealistic appeals, trusting rather to the arguments of what he called common sense. But, perhaps for that very reason, people would often take much from him which they would not have taken from more prophetic and enthusiastic lips. Certainly he was far better known, and more fully respected, when the Armistice was signed than he had ever been before. . . .

He had a profound belief in Providence; in God's working through history. Therefore he regarded the ordered sequence of events as of the most serious import. 'The Lord reigneth', he used constantly to say. This kept him calm and firm amid the turmoil, and also made him deem those who took the second step before they were sure of the first, in some particular course of action, as not only foolish but irreverent. A favourite text was 'One generation shall praise Thy works unto another'. Once, preaching on this text about Archbishop Whitgift, he said, 'In the life of a man, from boyhood to old age, some parts may be, and certainly will be, more stirring, more eventful, than others; but each bit has to do – quite necessarily and clearly – with what went before and what comes after. . . . God has had a purpose in moulding that life, personal or national bit by bit, and to His all-seeing eye each little epoch, each set of years, is concerned with all the rest, both past and future.' His instinctive approach to every subject was historical and evolutionary, and he saw every issue that came up as continuous with all else that had gone before it. Again and again he took the view that if people understood how a state of things had come to be, they would see what the next right step was. And when he stressed the evolutionary in history, it was always in terms rather of God's action than of mere development. We might not be able to see the relation between the little issues confronting each one of us and the plan of the Great Commander, but such a relation there always was. And his own sense of the importance of most of the things he was given to deal with was, at least in large measure, a sense of their ultimate importance in God's purpose (Bell, 1935, pp. 1152, 1166–7).

A2. Davidson had his own policy, which he pursued with tenacity and patience. It may have been both wise and necessary, but those who esteemed him most would hardly assert that it was either spectacular or heroic. Lang made that policy his own. From the outset he had resolved to render loyal collaboration, and for twenty years he kept his resolution so strictly that he was, as Dr Bell has written, 'the closest counsellor and the most trusted of all' (Lockhart, 1949, pp. 289–90).

A3. Bishop Lunt, who was appointed to the see of Ripon in 1935, continued the tradition that had been maintained by the previous suffragan bishop – he was paternal in his approach.

His own background was the parish ministry, and when he became a bishop he was 'a parish priest writ large'. He became the shepherd of the diocesan family.

The centenary of the diocese

The public image of the diocese was that of a family rejoicing over its hundredth birthday; the centenary provided for the bishop a ready-made opportunity for stressing the unity and fellowship of the people in the church. The 1936 Annual Report included a foreword by the bishop in which he spoke of 'our membership one of another in the great diocesan family'.

Two main events marked the festival: the centenary service in the cathedral and the launching of an appeal for £150,000 for the extension of the church in new areas. The bishop saw both the past and future as parts of one continuing tradition. On the one hand there was reference to what had gone before, such as the address to the Diocesan Conference in May 1936 on 'The Growth of Diocesan Consciousness in the Past Fifty Years'; on the other hand the church faced the tasks of the future, particularly those concerned with the new housing developments. Both were important, as indicated by the bishop when he referred to the value of his meetings with the clergy and members of the parochial church councils: 'They [the meetings] have served a useful purpose in quickening and strengthening that sense that we are members one of another in a great Diocesan Family, which is going to be so valuable an asset to us in the large tasks that lie ahead of us.'

The image of the church in 1936 continued through the next few years: the appeal for funds was kept open, and the festivities were extended by the observance of the 101st birthday in 1937, and the 102nd in 1938; and in 1939 there were even greater plans afoot for the 'family gathering of the diocese'. The celebrations were focused on the cathedral, and familial language was used in reference to it: 'Our Cathedral is "home" to us', said the bishop in December 1937.

National events conspired to enhance the emphasis on the traditions of the past and the challenge for the future. The coronation of King George VI in 1937 featured prominently in diocesan life. Special services were held; arrangements were made about listening to the broadcast; scripts and explanations of the ceremony were made available; and publicity was given to the archbishop's 'Recall' to dedication and commitment.

One of the main avenues of dissemination of publicity about these matters was the official diocesan publication called the *Gazette*, and many of its pages were dominated by the writings of the bishop and the details of the plans about the festivities. The *Gazette* consisted of eight large pages; in addition there was another paper entitled the *Messenger* consisting of four large pages which was mainly intended for use as an inset for parish magazines. It included the same kind of material about the centenary but less official matter; it provided the bishop with an opportunity to speak more informally about diocesan life.

The Diocesan Conference met twice a year, and the venue oscillated between Ripon, Harrogate, and Leeds. The attendance in this period rose from about 300 to 500, and this may indicate a growing sense of diocesan loyalty. No strong line of policy was indicated in the minutes; no mention was made of the content of the bishop's addresses, but they may well have followed the direction of his letters in the publications. Diocesan business was routine in terms of receiving reports and appointing committees; and a number of matters of general interest were introduced by various speakers.

Providing for population movements

One of the challenges that Bishop Lunt had to face was the extensive increase in population. New estates were being built very rapidly in various outlying parts of Leeds, and the needs of the people in those areas were very great. The main initiative came from a voluntary body, the Leeds Church Extension Society, founded in 1863 and with a long history to its credit. It undertook the responsibility for the selection of sites and for the planning and construction of the appropriate buildings; as a result of the efforts of the society, two new churches were built in 1935, two in 1938, and a further two in 1939. The earlier projects were financed by various generous donors and from the proceeds of the appeal launched by Bishop Burroughs called the Church Forward Movement. The response to this fund had been adversely affected by the depression years, so that by 1936 only £44,000 had been received instead of the expected £100,000.

Bishop Lunt therefore seized the opportunity that the centenary of the diocese provided and launched the new appeal which yielded sufficient funds for the churches which were built in this period. This enabled effect to be given, as stated in the 1937 Annual Report, to the 'determination not to allow the thousands of our people who are being moved into new housing areas to go wholly unshepherded by the Church: new Churches have got to be built'. Although the Leeds Church Extension

Society took the lead, the bishop provided for a general oversight of proceedings by the formation at the end of 1935 of the Bishop's Co-ordinating Committee which met eight or nine times a year during this period under review. It dealt with many different matters, but its main emphasis was pointed out by the bishop at the time of its demise in 1940; he said it was created 'purely as an Advisory body with which the Bishop could consult, and whose purpose was to co-ordinate the work of the various Executive bodies holding different responsibilities in Leeds and in the Diocese in relation to the building of new Churches'. A significant step in the history of the committee took place early in 1938 when the two main funds, the Church Forward Movement and the Bishop's Centenary Fund, were amalgamated into the Ripon Centenary Forward Movement, with the organizing secretary of the earlier fund taking over the running of both.

These financial arrangements were made independently of, though with the knowledge of, the Board of Finance, and this illustrates the general role played by the board in this period. By virtue of its articles of association, the board had complete control of the finances of the diocese; but each society and committee was free to pursue its own policies and to handle its own funds even when these were provided by the board. The board made annual allocations to those bodies which were constituted under its aegis but there was little supervision or control.

The committees on the church's mission

The Missionary Council acted quite independently, in keeping with the policy of the various missionary societies which resisted pressure to bring them on the national level under the general umbrella of the church's central financial machinery. Appeals from missionary societies were made in the parishes without any specific reference to the Board of Finance. The Missionary Council was responsible for assisting in these appeals and for the conduct of its own affairs even though it had a modest allowance from the board. The council sponsored missionary activities such as the visit of deputations and the dissemination of information and literature. It met only twice a year but in between these meetings an executive dealt with detailed business; in addition there was a sub-committee for Leeds which was mainly concerned with staging a missionary exhibition each year. A further development was the appointment of an Education Sub-committee for the organization of weekend missionary campaigns, the planning of missionary teaching, and co-ordination with other schemes of evangelism and education in the diocese.

The Moral Welfare Council also had a budget allowance from the Board of Finance from which allocations were made to various institutions and caseworkers. The social work was brought more into the picture by its association with diocesan celebrations and the establishment of a Women's Offering Appeal in 1938. Again this was with the permission of the Board of Finance but all the arrangements for the collection and distribution were done by the council. The main body of committees concerned with the mission of the church came under the general supervision of the Education Council. This body had its powers given to it from the Board of Finance as well as its financial allowance, but thereafter acted in the interests of promoting education in all its forms. Under the council were a number of committees: the Elementary Education Committee, the Higher Education Committee, the Leeds Elementary Education Sub-committee, the Adult Education Committee, and the Sunday School Committee. The function of the council was to serve them by supervising their constitutions, maintaining their membership, and overseeing their finances. The council also appointed representatives to a number of outside bodies concerned with education. Each committee pursued its own business appropriate to its title. The council thus operated in relation to its committees in a similar way to what the Board of Finance did in relation to the council and other bodies such as the Missionary Council and the Moral Welfare Council.

The Board of Finance

The Board of Finance, however, had a stronger relationship with other committees under its aegis. For instance, the Dilapidations Board had the same membership as the board and it held its meetings usually on the same day. This body dealt with the maintenance of vicarages and generally acted on the advice of the diocesan surveyor and a sub-committee. There was also the Church Buildings Committee which disbursed grants from the Board of Finance to churches in need of repair. Another body dealing with churches, but quite separate from the Board of Finance, was the Bishop's Advisory Committee on the Protection of Churches – the main people on the committee were the suffragan bishop and the two archdeacons. They were responsible for advising the chancellor of the diocese regarding any proposed alterations in the fabric of churches. They received applications for faculties but the issue of faculties was the chancellor's duty; if necessary, a parish had the right of access direct to him. The committee had a completely independent existence through these years with a steady stream of business to be dealt with.

Closer to the Board of Finance were committees such as the Publications Committee and the Clergy Stipends Committee; also in 1936 there were several others – the Trusts, Investments, and Administration sub-committees which were merged in 1937 into a General Purposes Committee which dealt with the business of the board in between its quarterly meetings. The board, in turn, virtually served as the executive committee of the Diocesan Conference in between its half-yearly gatherings.

The organizational character of the period

The Board of Finance represented the spearhead of classical organization structure penetrating the basic traditional pattern of the diocese. It had all the constitutional and financial authority in the diocese, but its power was not used in a way which put it in a controlling position. The working of the diocese had not become rationalized: the traditional forces were still dominant.

The diocese was a whole with many parts: some parts were constitutional and closely associated with the Board of Finance; others were more loosely under its wing; some bodies were voluntary and stood outside the constituted machinery; others were advisory; another was co-ordinating. There was clearly no rigid pattern of organization yet all served their several purposes very much on their own initiative and all cohered within the continuing life of the church. The diocese had to face changes – the environment was not completely static – and so as each new need was perceived, it was met by the response of a voluntary or official body or by the special creation of a particular body – hence the appeal of 1936, the action of the Leeds Church Extension Society, the formation of the Education Sub-committee of the Missionary Council. As each new part grew, it was merged into the general traditional pattern of the diocese; and even when the anomalies of multiplicity became obvious, the new situations were met in a similar way – the Co-ordinating Committee of 1935, the emergence of the General Purposes Committee of 1937, the amalgamation of funds in 1938 – and these new bodies, far from being a rationalization of the situation, were welded into the dominant traditional pattern.

The bishop's main emphasis was upon coherence and continuity in the family life of the diocese; he stressed the great occasions such as the centenary as the basis for thanksgiving for the past and hope for the future. The goals of the church were never made explicit – they were assumed, and it was assumed that they were shared by all. All that was needed was encouragement and nurture. The bishop's pastoral role predominated; and the character of diocesan machinery was such that it was possible to handle that aspect of diocesan life with the same paternal and traditional approach.

The period thus had a consistent pattern; the diocesan life was strong – strong enough to meet the demands foreshadowed by the clouds of war (Rudge, 1966a, pp. 198–208, slightly adapted).

A4. A minister and his wife on a visit to England from another country were invited to stay with their friends, the parish priest and his wife, in the rectory of a secluded little village. It was an attractive scene. The large stone rectory was at the foot of the driveway, nestling close to the ancient parish church. The cottages in the village lined the several narrow streets: all were in good order, well kept, and brightly painted. Around the village was a pleasant green countryside, dotted with trees, but somewhat exposed to the elements. Here and there were several large country homes including that of the lady of the manor.

The first impression was of the quietness of the village – little noise, no rush or bustle, only an occasional vehicle passing by. Everybody seemed to have time to spare. Life in the rectory was pleasant and gracious, though slightly on the frugal side. The rectory couple had only modest means, and there was a drain on their resources in sending their children to notable public schools. The rectory was so large as to be beyond the capabilities of the wife on her own; but she had assistance several days a week from a widow in the village. This woman's husband had worked on the estate and had occupied a small cottage in the village; the widow was allowed to retain the residence after his death on condition that she spent several mornings each week helping the rector's wife. The size of the rectory was reduced by the fact that part had been made into a self-contained flat; this was done before the arrival of the new rector but he inherited the account for about £1,000, the burden of which was offset slightly by the small rental from the tenants. The size of the house and the somewhat chilly climate made great demands on the antiquated heating plant; and a considerable part of the vicar's time was spent in nurturing this wayward instrument. And then he had a car – one of the few in the village – but of course the rector was always wealthy! And at the behest of the lady of the manor and at his own expense he used to drive the village people around.

On the arrival of the visitors, the rector informed the lady of their presence. It was agreed that the priest be invited to preach on the following Sunday; and the lady graciously invited the two visitors to her home. The engagement was kept, and they were duly entertained to dinner in a huge baronial dining hall where the butler attended to their needs. Following this, the second family in the district was informed; and the widowed lady of this house acted as a charming hostess at high tea.

Sunday came, with the morning service at 11 a.m. as it had been for centuries. The villagers duly took their accustomed seats in the nave of the church. They waited patiently for the arrival of the people of the manor house; and the rector paced in the porch. The lady and her husband were a few minutes late, but the service could not be started without their presence. At last they arrived and were escorted by the rector to their pew in the private chapel containing ancient tombs; and there they remained out of the sight of everybody. Meanwhile the chambermaid crept into the back pew of the nave. The distinguished couple received their communion first; and then the rest of the congregation came forward. At the end, all remained in their places until the lady and her husband emerged from their private retreat.

During the week the lady arranged a special function for the villagers. The visiting priest was asked to show some coloured slides at the village hall, and all the people were invited. The rector spent quite some time that day in getting the hall ready with seating, projector, and screen. The village people arrived in considerable numbers for the programme; they all took their accustomed places, leaving the third row of seats on the left for the people from the manorial hall. Unfortunately, the visiting wife, in her innocence, occupied one of these seats; but she was soon made to realize that this was where the lady sat.

In the course of conversation after the show, the priest and his wife were invited to visit another home nearby; the invitation was given by the secretary of an important lady who happened to be away at this time. The visitors gladly accepted; and reported this to their hosts on return to the rectory. The rector and his wife held up their hands in dismay – they had forgotten to ring this third family to tell them that there were guests at the rectory! (Rudge, original case.)

ILLUSTRATIONS OF THE CHARISMATIC THEORY

C1. One day, as Dick Sheppard and he [William Temple] sat talking in the Rectory study, Sheppard said with explosive suddenness, 'Don't you think, William dear, that there ought to be a "ginger" group in the Church?' . . . So began a Movement [the Life and Liberty Movement] that played a prominent part in English Church history during the next few years, and William Temple was its chosen leader and apostle. . . .

Among Sheppard's many gifts was the ability to recognize and seize for spiritual profit the opportunity of the passing hour. What H. G. Wells called 'gawdsakery' – 'for Gawd's sake do *something*' – was an impelling force in his life and work, and that the Church should 'get a move on' his most passionate desire; the particular form any movement might take, what and whom it was likely to involve, and whither it would lead – these were generally matters that would settle themselves as one went along. Never was this gift more valuable than in the early months of 1917. Here, he believed, was a veritable 'day of the Lord' such as prophets had proclaimed, when no venture of faith would go unrewarded, and when for those who felt the breath of the Spirit stirring through the Church no triumph was too splendid to be impossible. The National Mission had left the Church in a state of chastened discontent with itself, combined with a sense of frustration that baulked and halted all efforts towards a full recovery; the atmosphere was one of confusion in thought and purpose, and there was little to clear the air beyond a vague feeling that something ought to be done about it. It was one of those hours in which leaders emerge, who interpret the stammerings of the multitude, clear its head, give point to its purpose, and turn its aspirations into achievement. Quite certainly there was no definite plan in Sheppard's mind when he suggested to Temple the need of a 'ginger' group within the Church. His was merely the true instinct and, though he rightly believed that he could collect round him a number of sympathetic men and women whose influence was not negligible, he was also aware that he was not the man to work out the details of a practical policy or direct single-handed a far-reaching spiritual adventure. He therefore set to work in his own best way. Men and women, one after another in a long succession, were invited to his study, which they left with a firm impression that each had something of value to contribute to this new uprising in the Church; and the time came when he was ready to bring them all together round his table, where he believed that some definite plan would emerge from their discussions. But two things were missing – a leader and a programme. No deep thinking was required by Sheppard, or by any whom he had consulted, in the choice of a leader. There was only one man who seemed to possess all the qualities needed. Temple's work for the National Mission had brought him into close touch with every type of church member; comparatively few priests – and they were almost exclusively extreme Anglo-Catholics or extreme Erastians – did not trust him; and he could bring to the Movement a strength of mind and spirit that no one else could contribute. If with Sheppard's flashes of intuition and lively imagination were combined Temple's intellectual power, his wide knowledge, his ability in debate, and his charity in controversy, a strong rallying-point would be provided for the most forward-looking elements in the Church. And the programme? That would emerge from their meeting. . . . .

Temple was now thirty-six years old. He had a living of more than £2,000 a year; he was bound by close ties of affection to his parish, his church, and his staff; and his best work at S. James's was, almost certainly, to come. He was beginning to gather round him a thoughtful and sympathetic congregation, to whom he could speak from his pulpit with the freedom enjoyed only by a preacher who knows that he is both appreciated and understood. On the return of normal times he would have spare hours and days for his writing, and for helping the many societies and organizations that looked to him for guidance. He was already at the centre of church affairs, frequently consulted by the Archbishop, and able (since his election as a Proctor) to make his voice heard in Convocation. The commission he was asked to undertake for the Movement was a temporary one; at the end of two years he might find himself with no definite work, and longing for the post he had given up. Moreover, he had been married for only fifteen months and his wife had made for him the ordered home-life he loved and needed. Was he justified in asking her, already, to start a new home – where, he had no idea – on little more than a third of the income he was now receiving? It was a strong case.

On the other side were the dire need of the Church and his own wish to give himself, in complete surrender, to its service. The sacrifice hourly offered by men in the Forces was not being matched at home, least of all by the Church's leaders. But most of these were elderly men, whose lives were set – and set hard. To scarcely one of them was the 'incongruity of palaces and large incomes' at this moment in their country's history so immediately and distastefully obvious as it was to the men in the trenches and on the high seas. But Temple was of the age of the fighting men – he at least could see a picture of the Church through their eyes – and he sat more loosely to the world. Did he think back to his own constant appeals for sacrifice to those who had stayed at home? To the sermon he had preached in his own church on his return from America? And, above all, to that memorable night at the Queen's Hall and the message of the Spirit to the Church that he had then declared: 'Come out of your safety and comfort . . . listen to the voice of the wind as it sweeps over the world, and stand where you may be caught in its onward rush'? . . .

In the judgement of worldly-wise prelates and by the trivial standards of scheming men the whole project was quixotic, if not preposterous.

But – beyond question or dispute – *sub specie aeternitatis* there was no greater moment in Temple's life (Iremonger, 1948, pp. 219–21, 238–40).

C2. Burroughs was a man of intellectual brilliance and prophetic gifts. He was among those people in the 1930s who foresaw the impending world troubles and the shadows of war; and on these and other matters of wide concern he raised his prophetic voice. However, his approach to the episcopal office 'led him to embark upon enterprises outside the necessary routine work of the Diocese, the number and variety of which would have taxed the strongest constitution to the limit of endurance' (Malden, 1935, p. 31). Nevertheless he acted constructively in relation to a growing problem in his diocese. Population growth had been a major concern for earlier bishops; a different aspect was the changing distribution of the population, especially in Leeds. Burroughs appointed a commission in 1927 to explore the situation, and as a consequence the Church Forward Movement was inaugurated to cope with the new situation (Rudge, 1966a, pp. 193–4).

C3. The parish of Hollywood had an auspicious beginning in that the new church of St Hilary, consecrated in 1938, was the subject of an architectural prize. At that time the newly established housing estate of Hollywood in the suburbs of a large industrial city had a population of about 5,000, mostly people in the artisan class.

Twenty years later the population had grown to 8,000 or more, but the life of the church did not measure up to its imaginative architecture: no money had been spent on maintenance, and a report revealed a need to spend £5,000 on this; the income consisted of about £500 from direct giving and £500 from other sources; the attendance at the services was poor – twenty to thirty adults at matins and forty at evensong; there was virtually no leadership; few men gave their support; and the church played little part in the life of the community.

The new vicar who came in July 1959 described the situation as 'disconsolate'. He had been in the Church Army for seventeen years where his main emphasis had been on evangelism and social work; he was a dynamic personality; and the parish was a challenge to him. After surveying the situation in the first six months of his incumbency, he took steps to remedy the plight of the parish.

One plan was to hold a stewardship campaign which in the ensuing five years raised the income from £10 per week to £60 per week. This reflected a deeper change in the parish life.

The other main part of his programme was the introduction of the parish communion with the celebrant in the westward position. The vicar felt that the gathering of the people around the altar, emphasized by the priest's facing the people, could be the focus of a renewed parish life and of all parish strategy.

The existing roster of services provided for an early service of Holy Communion at 8 a.m. and matins at 11 a.m.; the vicar allowed these arrangements to stand and he scheduled the proposed new service to fit in between the others at 9.30 a.m. The proposal was discussed in the parish and at meetings of the Parochial Church Council; although there was some opposition, the new plan came into force in March 1960 to coincide with the first Sunday of the stewardship campaign.

The vicar felt that a new sense of parish life gradually grew out of the experience of the parish communion – 'something has happened' – and much took place in the parish which he considered was an extension of the essential commitment involved at this point, though prosperity depended on whether people caught the vision of the new order or not.

The development had an impact on the other services. Although it was not designed to replace either of the existing morning services, it began to have an adverse effect on the service of matins at 11 a.m. The numbers began to dwindle and eventually the choir refused to attend. The service was thus abandoned, though not till after eighteen months had elapsed.

The Sunday school experienced a difficult time. On his arrival the vicar found that it was virtually defunct but he attempted to revive it by incorporating it into the parish communion. Such a service lent itself to more participation than other services, and there was room for teaching within it. However, the experiment failed after about three months, and the Sunday school lapsed for a while.

Some parish organizations were adversely affected by the change in emphasis in parish life. Such were groups like the Church Lads' Brigade and the Girls' Friendly Society, which gradually dwindled in numbers and influence. These groups were held together by loyalty to their respective charters which governed the life of these bodies on virtually a national basis; these charters tended to be inflexible and did not necessarily allow for adaptability to new situations. Thus these bodies were organized somewhat independently of the new charter – that based on participation in the parish communion – which the vicar brought into the parish. The whole strength of his leadership was in the latter direction and so he virtually left the various societies without support.

On the other hand, groups which were established on the basis of the new order in the parish grew in size and influence. The young people's fellowship sprang up at the same time as the development of the parish communion and played a significant part in it. In the early stages, the young people comprised over half the congregation; they felt at home in a service which allowed their participation.

Among the adults who came to participate more and more in the parish communion were the young wives. Within eighteen months or so they began to make their presence felt in the congregation; they had come to appreciate the way in which they could bring their children with them without the fears or embarrassment that they would have felt at other services. These people developed their own parish organization which fostered their sense of belonging to the church; the growth was slow, but by 1965 they were firmly established with their own leaders.

Another significant feature was the increase in the number of candidates for confirmation, many of whom were men. There was a cumulative effect. The parish communion movement tended to attract new candidates and they, when they were confirmed, added to the strength of the parish communion (Rudge, 1966a, pp. 377–84, excerpts).

C4. It was the morning on which Sir Winston Churchill died. The announcement of his death was made soon after 8 a.m., and one of the churchwardens told the priest-in-charge of the news immediately before the 9 a.m. celebration during which appropriate bidding prayers were used. The priest-in-charge did not feel that he had time to change the sermon for the 10.45 a.m. service but thought of using suitable occasional prayers. Just before going into the service one of the churchwardens drew his attention to the fact that many people coming into the church had not heard the news, and so at the beginning of the service the priest-in-charge made the announcement; he indicated that references to Sir Winston would be made in the prayers, but otherwise the service would continue as usual. The news of Sir Winston's death was accompanied by a wave of emotion among the congregation, of which the priest-in-charge was aware; it made him realize in the course of the service that the use of prayers only would not be adequate – there was the need of something in which the people could express their feelings more openly. By an intuitive process, the priest-in-charge thought of the use of the national anthem and so he hurriedly wrote a note to the organist suggesting the three verses of this in place of the hymn after the third collect, the transposing of that hymn to the place before the sermon, and the abandoning of the proposed hymn for that place because it was not in keeping with the occasion. The organist nodded his assent and handed the note around the members of the choir so that they would be prepared. The priest-in-charge duly announced the national anthem, suggesting its appropriateness for the occasion and indicating that to some extent the verse beginning

O Lord our God, arise,
Scatter our enemies,
And make them fall;

expressed some of the fighting characteristics for which Sir Winston would be remembered. The anthem was sung and the appropriate prayers followed.

Afterwards in the vestry, one churchwarden made a remark to the effect that he felt that the choice of the national anthem was 'a stroke of inspiration'; the other objected to the use of 'Victorian jingoism' implicit in the verse to which the priest-in-charge particularly referred (Rudge, 1966a, pp. 503–4).

ILLUSTRATIONS OF THE CLASSICAL THEORY

X1. Although parliament still had the final say, the denominational machinery of the church was brought into being; but the new constitution had within it the seeds of a dilemma. Was the Church Assembly to deal with matters spiritual or material? Iremonger said (1948, p. 281): 'There was a sharp and fateful struggle between two groups in the National Church Assembly who differed widely in their conviction of its policy and its purpose and may be called, roughly, the legalists and the moralists.' He went on to say that the issue was soon resolved: 'the voice of the Assembly is now the voice of the administrator, not the prophet'. The charismatic Life and Liberty Movement ended in the creation of a bureaucracy.

This did not mean that the Assembly did not do its work well. Iremonger said (p. 281) that 'if it be granted that the object of the Assembly is to reorganize the administration and finances of the Church, its members deserve credit for many useful reforms which it might have taken two generations to effect under the old system of passing church Bills through Parliament'. These activities were amenable to being dealt with by classical methods, and although steps were taken towards democratizing church government, the church's civil service came to occupy an influential position, all the more so because this kind of government demanded qualities of leadership for which the bishops, by virtue of their total ethos of life, were generally unprepared (Rudge, 1966a, pp. 57–9).

X2. It was first of all required of both bishops and parish priests that they should be good administrators, for the whole process of centralization greatly multiplied the actual administration that they had to do. . . . The Church was gradually submerged under a cloudburst of prophecy and planning, of commissions and reports, of boards and committees with the organizations and officials in every diocese (Lloyd, 1946–50, II, 158–9).

X3. Post-war reorganization on the national side was anticipated in the field of education; particularly from 1942 onwards, the way was being prepared by R. A. Butler and James Chuter Ede all over the country for the 1944 Education Act to which Butler's name has been popularly attached since. This act reshaped the whole education programme of the country: it made provision in statutory terms for the church's part through aided or controlled schools; and it included provision for religious teaching in the syllabus. Both had far-reaching influence on diocesan arrangements.

All the time that the act was being foreshadowed, there was much activity in the diocese in relation to education. The Religious Education Council resumed its full meetings after the initial war phase and in 1942 it appointed a sub-committee to report on plans for the post-war period regarding what educational work should be undertaken and what changes would be necessary to achieve this. The report was presented in early 1944, and by this time the details of the Butler Education Act were known. The bishop took the chair for this important meeting and major decisions were made: a director and three assistants were appointed to deal with educational matters; the council was to become the statutory body under the act; as many schools as possible were to be retained for the church as aided schools; finance for these was to come from the Board of Finance and a special appeal; and attempts were to be made to revive the teaching office of a priest and to increase interest in Sunday schools and their teachers. Thereafter there was a considerable emphasis in meetings of the council on its statutory obligations, although much of the detailed work was done by the reconstituted Leeds Primary and Secondary Education Committee for schools in Leeds and by the reformed Primary Education Committee and Secondary Education Committee for other schools in the diocese. These two committees were combined into a Schools Committee in 1947.

The new act introduced new influences into the diocese. A large segment of decision-making in the diocese was now brought under statutory provisions, a situation which carried with it at least some of the implications of bureaucracy and government by regulation. The Board of Finance, as well as the particular committees, were bound by such provisions; there was also an emphasis on specialization and expertness: the officials of the council had to be more than amateurs in educational matters and in the understanding of the law.

The bringing of education in schools under direct statutory rule began to reveal the distinction between the formal and informal education in the diocese; the other committees under the aegis of the council dealt with the latter and were to some extent placed in an anomalous position because of the way in which the statutory education dominated the mind of the council. The Adult Education Committee continued its limited existence, carrying on such items as various series of lectures, and reporting from time to time to the council; the Sunday School Committee had its work brought more into the light by the question of the relation of its work to that now being done in schools, but no major developments took place (Rudge, 1966a, pp. 219–21).

X4. The Board of Finance became the financial agent for the Diocesan Reorganization Committee when it was formed in 1941 under a measure of Church Assembly, and this set the trend for the board through this period. In 1941 also, on the initiative of the Church Commissioners, the board commenced a survey of diocesan resources. In 1943–44, at the peak of the discussions of post-war reorganization, the board conducted an inquiry into the condition of the small parishes of the diocese and acted as adviser on the other consequences of the various proposals. Thoughts were turned to the post-war needs of the diocese and its committees; a budget was proposed in 1943, and in 1944 the secretary was asked to report on the post-war requirements of the committees and to guide the conference about these. These figures were available in 1945. The secretary anticipated the development of appeals, and in the immediate post-war days he was engaged in co-ordinating that appeal launched by the bishop and the one sponsored by the archbishops. In addition, the board had a new role under the Education Act. The total effect of all these matters was that the work of the board, and particularly of the secretary, increased considerably: he felt the pressure imposed by the new legislation under which he had to operate. The work was more complex, and financial expertness was needed to understand and simplify the accounts. Plans for reorganization were to a large degree dependent on the appropriate financial measures being taken, and the various committees were gradually being brought under the growing dominance of financial government (Rudge, 1966a, pp. 222–3).

X5. In the midst of the changing fortunes of the various committees, the Board of Finance became stronger and stronger. A highly rationalized and conscious budget procedure had developed out of the financial measures taken in the later war phase; and the decisions of the board were the determining factors in diocesan life. The board exercised a much greater control over spending by committees, very largely because of financial stringency; every item had to be weighed. There was still the democratic process in operation; representatives of the committees met informally with the secretary of the Board of Finance to make known their requirements, and the budget was ultimately accepted by the representatives of parishes at the Diocesan Conference. Nevertheless, the officials of the board played a very large part in the decision-making process. At the board meetings (again of members who were elected), the secretary played a major role. One person caricatured the meetings as 'an opening prayer by the bishop and a monologue by the secretary'. Circumstances conspired to place the Board of Finance in a dominant position in diocesan life so that the bishop himself had to accede to this situation at least for the time being (Rudge, 1966a, pp. 235–6).

X6. The Pastoral Committee began its work in 1950, and its first task was with the country rural deaneries in turn; then the city of Leeds became the focus of attention. In the meantime some steps had been taken to deal with the particular needs of growing areas on the lines laid down earlier, and there was support in this field from the New Housing Areas (Church Buildings) Measure, 1954, under which the Pastoral Committee operated. The Church Building Committee was also brought into the considerations. For some time the building of dual purpose halls was in favour, but gradually the emphasis changed to the erection of permanent churches; this building programme began to get under way in this period with new churches at Moor Allerton in 1954 and at Seacroft in 1956.

The focus of attention on the overall situation in Leeds dated from the end of 1951, and special consideration was given to the centre of the city and the depopulated areas. In 1953 and 1954 much time was spent in gathering information about the population movements and the proposed development of the city centre. A sweeping plan for the centre was produced, and one part of it, the proposal to sell or demolish Holy Trinity Church in Boar Lane, became the issue in a controversy on a national scale. It was eventually gazetted by the Ministry of Works as a building of historical value, and this closed the issue. The Church Commissioners, in considering the proposal, made an alternative recommendation that the Pastoral Committee consider the problem in relation to a full survey of the whole city. A small sub-committee then worked on these lines and produced a comprehensive report in 1956. It dealt with sensible boundary adjustments within the central part of the city and in areas that had been depopulated; and by means of consultation with and co-operation by incumbents and parochial church councils, a number of anomalies were straightened out. The report also provided a basis for a more comprehensive approach to the developing areas.

Being a statutory committee, the Pastoral Committee had a considerable standing in the executive side of diocesan affairs, and in this period took over, to some extent, the dominant role that the other statutory body, the Board of Finance, had in the preceding phase [X5, p. 88]. The main initiative in the diocese was in the hands of the Pastoral Committee. In its early days it had taken to itself work that had belonged to former bodies dealing with reorganization; it had also taken over responsibility from the Board of Finance in respect to stipends, which were dealt with by the Maintenance and Pensions Committee. A further development in the same direction was the establishment of a Ways and Means Committee in 1955; it performed the function of being an executive to the policy-making Pastoral Committee. To give effect to the decisions of the Pastoral Committee, the Ways and Means Committee had to deal in finance and consider how the new buildings programme was to be paid for. It also acted as a sub-committee for the parent body in collecting information and formulating policy; and it came to do so more and more. The frequency of the meetings of the Pastoral Committee dropped from eight or nine times a year to five or six times a year after 1955; and it came to rely more on the recommendations presented to it. The few on the Ways and Means Committee were responsible for all decision-making; and this function virtually fell into the hands of one man. The Pastoral Committee in this period took over not only many of the functions of the Board of Finance, but also the character of the decision-making process of the board in the previous period (Rudge, 1966a, pp. 240–2).

X7. Prior to his arrival in the village parish, the new vicar (in his first incumbency) read the copies of the parish magazine for the previous eighteen months, looked through the parish registers, and talked to the former incumbent. He was inducted and instituted on Friday, July 31; and the ceremony was followed by a reception and welcome. He began his ministry with the services on Sunday, August 2; he had previously asked that the normal programme be rearranged so that there would be parish communion at 9.15 a.m. instead of the 8 a.m. celebration and the 10.30 a.m. matins.

The parish magazine which was published at this time included a letter from the new vicar in which he spoke of his hopes of meeting the people (perhaps in groups in houses) and of his general convictions about the life of the church. He was concerned with the mission of the church and felt that all church activities should be a preparation for this.

The month of August, his first month in the parish, was part of the summer recess, and there was little activity in the church apart from Sunday services. The vicar wanted to use this time in getting to know the situation and meeting the key people. He was thwarted in the latter because many people were away at this time on holidays; moreover the last two weeks of the month were occupied by the local village fair. By contrast, the month of September was a time of intense activity: all organizations of the church came to life again, and there was a full programme of events.

August

The vicar continued the schedule of Sunday services with no major alterations except that on the first Sunday, but he made changes in the services by transposing the sermon and the occasional prayers at matins and evensong. He explained this action in retrospect in the September magazine by saying that he had done this so 'that the theme brought out in the sermon can be the subject of the prayers, and the congregation can more easily enter into the spirit of them. The prayers are offered in the body of the church because they are the prayers of the people.' On one occasion the congregation adjourned after the third collect into the parish hall to see a film, and the vicar indicated in the August magazine that he might experiment with such teaching methods in association with the sermon. Another small change was to move the font to the front of the nave below the chancel steps for the services of baptism.

Particularly in the first week the vicar spent much time in finding out about the plant and equipment in the parish. On the first Monday he went through all the papers and files in the office; on Tuesday he looked around the parish hall and checked on the lighting; and on Friday he had an interview with the church cleaner; early in the next week he examined the stewardship records; later in the month he spent a morning looking through the linen and vestments.

Another preoccupation was his meeting with the key laymen in the parish and those in the church organizations. His programme of consultations was as follows:

3 Tuesday	Group scoutmaster *re* youth club and uniformed groups
6 Friday	Sunday school and kindergarten superintendents
	Churchwardens
10 Monday	Sunday school teachers
13 Thursday	Leaders of the Mothers' Union
	Church secretary
18 Tuesday	Christian stewardship leaders
26 Wednesday	Uniformed leaders
27 Thursday	Men's fellowship leaders
28 Friday	Diocesan stewardship adviser

These meetings were not just to gain information but to determine policy. The vicar's idea was that the organizations should be a real part of the church fellowship and that the whole congregation should be aware of their existence and function; the organizations should also be the nucleus of the missionary work of the church, and their programmes should include training for this. That the vicar should be concerned with policy surprised the leaders; they had been accustomed to forming their own plans and going ahead with them.

What transpired from these meetings was that the stewardship anniversary would be held on October 22, to which all those with links with the church would be invited and at which the organizations would give a display of their aims. Another point was that the uniformed groups should be distinctive church bodies with the vicar participating in their leadership. The Sunday school situation was examined carefully, and as a result a course of instruction for the teachers was planned for the Wednesday nights in September and October with a view to strengthening the staff so as to provide more adequately for the children.

On the pastoral side there were some matters of an ordinary nature: the vicar paid several visits to the sick in hospital and home; there were several funerals, some couples to prepare for marriage, and some normal calls to make. In addition he spent some time compiling a document on confirmation which was printed and circulated; notice of its contents was also given in the magazine. The date for the service was set for May 28 next, and he called for candidates both young and old. He promised to hold three classes, one for each age group – school children, youth, and adults; and the classes would continue until the confirmation.

There was also a considerable amount of routine office work: correspondence, registers, and records. He prepared material for the next parish magazine, and this occupied most of Tuesday, August 18, and Wednesday evening, August 19; and part of the following day was spent at the publishers. To help with the work, he formed a small magazine committee. A survey of magazine readers was planned and conducted in September to find out their views and suggestions.

The vicar had some outside links and appointments: he was visited by a neighbouring vicar, the local Methodist superintendent, the Congregational minister, and the Roman Catholic curate. He had some free time at home; and he also had the opportunity to visit the nearby city on several occasions and to go away for a wedding.

September

The month of September was marked by the commencement of church activities; and the full programme of meetings was determined partly by the normal pattern of parish life and partly by the decisions of the vicar in the previous month. The fixed appointments for the month were:

1	Tuesday	Sunday school teachers
2	Wednesday	Stewardship Continuation Committee
6	Sunday	8.00 Holy Communion
		10.30 Matins
		11.30 Holy Communion
		2.15 Sunday school
		6.30 Evensong
		Youth fellowship
7	Monday	Mothers' Union opening
8	Tuesday	Social Services Committee
9	Wednesday	Teacher training course
13	Sunday	8.00 Holy Communion
		10.30 Matins
		2.15 Sunday school
		3.30 Baptisms
		6.30 Evensong
16	Wednesday	Teacher training course
17	Thursday	Fraternal meeting of local clergy of various denominations
19	Saturday	Diocesan missionary exhibition and workshop
20	Sunday	9.30 Parish Communion

	11.30 Matins
	2.15 Sunday school
	6.30 Evensong
21 Monday	Parochial Church Council
23 Wednesday	Teacher training course
26 Saturday	Annual meeting of the Church Pastoral Aid Society
27 Sunday	8.00 Holy Communion
	10.30 Matins
	2.15 Sunday school
	3.30 Baptisms
	6.30 Evensong
29 Tuesday	Men's fellowship
30 Wednesday	Teacher training course

In addition there were meetings for the magazine committee, the scout parents' committee, the church hall committee, the choir on Thursdays (which he seldom attended); and in the future there would be the three weekly meetings for confirmation preparation. The stewardship committee and its preparations for the function in October also occupied a considerable amount of time. As there was no caretaker, the vicar had further duties regarding the cleaning of the hall and the handling of bookings, but he did not give much time to these matters.

Impressions

Some of the vicar's impressions at the end of the second month are worth noting.

He felt a need for a regular pattern of services instead of the anomalous programme on the third Sunday; he hoped that there would be a fixed time every Sunday for the main service, perhaps at 10 a.m. There were tentative plans for a regular parish communion to start in January.

He felt that he had come to know the inner circle of people very well but not many beyond them; the pressure of other things had ruled out the suggestion of house meetings, and he realized that the pressure was increasing; his evenings were being filled with appointments of a regular nature. The limitation on outside contacts meant that he was less able to see whether the pattern of parish life was meeting the real needs of the community. A survey conducted by some of the professional class in the congregation (these people did not attend the usual parish organizations) in the previous régime had been somewhat abortive in that few saw the point of it; the magazine questionnaire did not go very deep. The vicar also saw that some parish activities clashed with the other commitments that young people had at night school: church meetings only added to their burdens.

The vicar was disappointed that the Parochial Church Council did not take a more responsible role in parish life. At the meeting in September there was silent approval for his plans but no active or concerned discussion. The council's outlook was virtually limited to items of management and finance. Another concern of the vicar was the amount of time spent on office work; he felt he was involved too much in filing records, in sorting out stewardship details, in channelling information that rightly should have gone to secretaries of organizations, and in the management of the hall.

His final comments were: 'The policy of making the organizations more oriented towards training has not been welcomed. They don't want anything too religious!' (Rudge, 1966a, pp. 307–15.)

ILLUSTRATIONS OF THE HUMAN RELATIONS THEORY

Y1. The second phase of Bishop Chase's episcopate saw something of the fruition of his original hopes. In the first stage [X5, p. 88], the role of administrator was predominant partly because of the pressures within diocesan organization and partly because of the need for action in this field. But the bishop never accepted this as the permanent direction of diocesan life: he was concerned with pastoral and democratic ideals; he felt that the diocese should have a life of its own, and likewise all the parts should have initiative and responsibility; he wanted people to do things themselves; he sought out leaders to take over the various aspects of the work – and so behind the image that he presented in the earlier part of his episcopate he was quietly working towards a different emphasis in the character of the diocese.

He went on an American tour for the last half of 1952 and this event as much as anything provided the basis for dating the change in emphasis in diocesan life. The change was most noticeable in the public image of the diocese.

The format of the publications was altered. The *Messenger* ceased in August 1952 on the departure of its editor and for financial reasons. In its place the bishop wrote a monthly letter which was duplicated and sent to editors of parish papers for inclusion in these. The *Gazette* was reduced in size but not in the number of pages; and it was placed in the hands of a new editor at the beginning of 1953. Although it was stated in the last issue of 1952 that 'this is a leadership organ, rather than a magazine for all and sundry', the latter view eventually prevailed. The new editor often said in the paper: 'We hope readers will submit articles and letters. We want the *Gazette* to be a forum for considered opinion.' In the next few years it contained less of formal diocesan material and more of personal contributions on a wide range of topics with varying degress of relationship to the task and purpose of the church. The bishop contributed less and less to the official publication; his letter became 'The Bishop's Notes'; instead he used the informal duplicated letter. What was more significant was his change of emphasis from written to personal communication; his pastoral concerns were expressed by more immediate contacts than the written word. There was also a marked change in the character of the Diocesan Conference. No longer was there the dominance of proceedings by the business of the diocese; financial affairs did not occupy the centre of attention. Considerable time was given to reports from the various committees, and more room was provided for their contributions. The bishop displayed his pastoral touch by referring to the personnel of the diocese: newcomers, new appointments, resignations, and transfers. Towards the end of his episcopate he made some valuable scholarly contributions to the conferences on the history of canon law, the question of the death penalty, and the Wolfenden report. A large part of the time was spent on the consideration of topics of wide and general interest though with no clear pattern or relation to a definite goal – the ministry of music, the care of the deaf and dumb, the Evanston conference, the church overseas. Interest, however, was maintained, and there was a consistent attendance of about 300 people throughout (Rudge, 1966a, pp. 238–40).

Y2. The former individualist-sacramentalist approach depended on the maintaining of a certain ratio of priests and people; but this has proved to be impossible because of the shortage of clergy (and the means to pay them) and because of the large increase of the population in the parish.

The individualist emphasis has been replaced by the stress on the corporate nature of the nucleus of committed Christians; the ministry of the church is by this corporate body and not just by the clergy; and the grace of God is found through sharing in the experience of this togetherness instead of in a rather mechanistic participating in the sacraments. Corresponding to this policy there can be a consistent pattern of parish life. The communion is still taken to the incapacitated; but there is a feeling that in some cases such ministrations are merely mechanical both for the priest and for the communicant – and so what was meant as a pastoral operation has ceased to be so.

The weekday services have been reduced in number; and to some extent they are regarded as places where the committed nucleus of people meet. The staff celebrations on Thursdays are a special case of this, the team of clergy being a vital part of the inner group. No longer are the clergy isolated individuals in separate areas; they meet together as a group; and vicar and curates are on an equal footing.

The general pattern of services on Sundays has been continued; but the emphasis in the parish communion is on sharing together. The adoption of the westward position enhances this; children come to the communion rail to be blessed at the time of the administration; at times the Sunday school children are incorporated into the service; the fellowship of the service is extended to the social gathering over a cup of tea or coffee after the service. The parish communion type of service is often used for patronal and other festivals; and the team of clergy all participate in the liturgy on these occasions.

Such an emphasis in worship has necessitated changes in architectural features. Alterations in the sanctuary have been made at St Richard's and St James's; only St Luke's was originally designed with the westward position in view. *Ad hoc* provisions have had to be made at St Luke's for the social gathering after the service because the building was not fitted out for this; at the Ascension, there has to be an adjournment to the nearby hall; at St James's use is made of the facilities of the youth room in the adjacent building; social area can be screened off at St Richard's and there is a kitchen there.

The parish organizations which have hitherto existed have been given comparatively little attention because their charters – whether of the Mothers' Union, or scouts and guides, or money-raising groups – are not closely and specifically related to the concept of the caring nucleus. Those that are related to this concept are given much more attention. St Richard's Ladies is one example of this kind of group – they seem to be geared very closely to this conception of parish life. There are other groups, too, most of which meet in clergy houses or in private homes; this obviates the need for a large hall; what is needed is a small and convenient meeting place. These groups are study groups or confirmation classes for adults; there is no longer any stress on mustering huge batches of young confirmation candidates.

The caring ministry of the church has been in relation to those in particular need. Some of this caring has been done by the clergy who have eschewed a widespread campaign of visiting and have concentrated on meeting needs either through special calls or through people calling on them. Some of these contacts are related to baptism, marriage, bereavement; but whatever the issue, the ministry is in terms of caring and meeting needs for the sake of the people without any 'spiritual blackmail' about getting people to church. A considerable counselling ministry has been developed; but at none of the churches is there an adequate interview room, although some steps have recently been taken at St Richard's to put the vestry into suitable shape. Only two residences, Mr Short's and Mr Raven's, have appropriate facilities; the vicar has to use the lounge in his house; Mr Cherry has to do likewise, with his wife excluded from her own private rooms and with clients queueing up outside in cars.

The caring ministry is also exercised by the committed laity though this is not generally known. The issue has been raised in recent discussions about area stewards who were envisaged – in the Wells report, in the guide book for the stewards, and in the minds of many on the church committees and continuation committees – as an extension of the kind of ministering envisaged in the former policy. In two instances at least, it has been publicly stated by clergymen that in fact there are many area stewards already in operation but in terms of the caring nucleus policy.

The fact that this kind of development of area wardens was news to those who had the general responsibility for church government points to perhaps the most serious difficulty in operating according to the caring nucleus policy: that the vital decisions about ministering are made in groups – of laity, of clergy and laity together, and of the clergy as a team – whereas those entrusted with the continuing government of the church do not really know what is being done in the ministering area and continue to make provision for the ministering on the lines of the previous policy (Rudge, 1966b, pp. 3–5, excerpts).

Y3. Gopherwood was a small village in a rural area; it had its own church, and although the parish was united with the neighbouring Gopherville, the vicar lived at Gopherwood. He found the tempo of life much different from what he knew in his previous city parish but he adapted readily to it, partly because of his upbringing in the country.

Although the pattern of church life was conservative, he wanted to introduce something of the widespread thinking on the liturgy to his people. In the middle of 1964 he found four members of the Parochial Church Council who were interested, and at his instigation they were appointed by the council on July 29 as a Liturgical Committee. They had no powers beyond the collecting of information and the making of suggestions:

> This small committee's task is simply to look into our present pattern of Sunday worship to see if it would be advisable to make any alterations. In the course of time I am hoping it will look not only at the

times of our services: but at the type of service – its content and such things as the possibility of increased lay participation, the sort of music we have, whether more or fewer prayers should be said together by all and so on.

The committee met for the first time on November 17, and the discussion was preceded by the vicar's reading the foreword by the Archbishop of York to the book *Re-shaping the Liturgy* which had been recently published by the Church Information Office. He did this, as he put it in his own words, 'to show them that what I was asking them to consider was part of a very much bigger movement which is taking place not only in the Church of England, but in other parts of the Anglican Communion and indeed other Christian Communions too, e.g. the Roman Catholics'. Several matters arose out of the evening's discussion. One was a recommendation to be passed on to the council for its next meeting on December 3 that there should be greater lay participation in the services. A suggestion was that the lessons at matins and evensong be read by laymen at the vicar's discretion; the members were insistent that only competent people should be invited to read. Another opportunity was the reading of the epistle at the 9.30 a.m. or 11 a.m. communion, again at the vicar's discretion; but members objected to the idea of having a layman to read the gospel.

The committee also considered the question of the times of services, and the result was the preparation of the following questionnaire which was issued on the next Sunday:

Questions on the time of morning service

Please answer the following questions and return your answer *by next Sunday* if possible or *Sunday week at the latest.*
Your answers can be handed to the Vicar, posted to him, or placed in the box provided for the purpose in church.

1. Are you satisfied with the present time of Morning Service? If not, at what other time would you prefer it?

   ....

2. Would you accept the 1st 2 Sundays at 11 a.m. and the 3rd, 4th, and 5th Sundays at 9.30 a.m.
   (a) All the year round? or
   (b) In the summer only?

Another project of interest was the attempt to understand why those who came to church infrequently did not come more often and why others did not come at all. A request was then formulated for the council that each councillor be asked to elicit from two people well known to him why they did not come or only came infrequently. Answers were to be written down and handed in to the vicar within a fortnight of the next meeting.

The council met on December 3 and considered the first of the recommendations; however, it turned down the idea of greater lay participation in the services. The vicar forgot to mention the last suggestion of eliciting information about non-churchgoing; and no action could be taken on the main issue of the proposed questionnaire as the results were not in at that time.

Seventy-four questionnaire forms were taken from the church and, of these, forty-four were returned by December 13. From these the vicar analysed the results and produced the following report for the Liturgical Committee which met on December 16:

Answers to Question 1:

34 answered 'Yes'	(of these, 2 preferred 10.30; 1 was 'not strongly opposed to 9.30')
6 implied 'No'	(of these, 5 said 9.30)
4 did not answer the question	
44	

Answers to Question 2:

16 answered 'Yes'	(of these, 11 said 'Yes' to 2a, 'all the year round'; 4 said 'Yes' to 2b, 'summer only'; 1 said 'Yes' to 2a and 2b)
10 implied 'No'	(of these, 6 said 'No'; 3 crossed the question out; 1 said 'at a fixed time all the year round')
18 did not answer the question	
44	

These findings were subsequently published in the February newsletter in addition to being presented to the committee. The committee saw the answers as a clear indication that the majority were satisfied with the present times of the morning service, and no change was recommended.

However, the committee considered a number of items concerning worship other than the actual times of services. The topics and the findings were:

1. Should Communion be more frequent than at present?

Yes. Matins should be monthly instead of fortnightly, but the

Canticles sung at Matins should be included at Communion from time to time.

2. Should more or fewer prayers be said together than at present?

Our present practice should continue (that is, of saying together the Collect for Purity, the Prayer of Humble Access, and the Prayer of Thanksgiving, or Oblation).

3. How much should we say and/or sing, e.g. The Creed?

The Creed should be said on ordinary Sundays but sung at Festivals.
The 'Gloria' should always be sung. Omit the 'Gradual' hymn.
Organ music should be soft after end of service at Communion or Matins.
Psalms should be said.
Choir should recess during the last hymn at Communion.

4. On the use of silence during our worship.

There should be a longer period of silence after the end of the Consecration Prayer at Communion. Also retain the silence after the 3rd Collect at Matins and Evensong as at present.

The next meeting of the committee was scheduled for January 27, 1965, but it was postponed partly because of a bereavement involving two members of the group. A further factor leading to the delay was the impending discussion of the material entitled 'No Small Change' provided by the Church of England Board of Education for use in parishes during Lent; it was designed to involve the people in the discussion of implications of the programme of Mutual Responsibility and Interdependence.

Early in Lent, discussions began in several groups of parishioners, and as a result of a meeting of leaders on March 7 a document was produced entitled 'The Parish Looks at its Purpose'. It listed a number of points under headings such as Evangelism, Social Action and Service, and Education. Another of the topics was Worship, the subject which had hitherto been the responsibility of the Liturgical Committee. The document included questions on various points, and people were asked to think and pray about these matters. Copies were circulated to parishioners with the April newsletter. Attention was drawn to the importance of the questions in the sermons on Easter Day; in the May newsletter the vicar added: 'I view your co-operation in this matter as being of the greatest possible importance for the future life of our Church in this Parish.' He requested that answers to the questions be handed in by Sunday, May 2, so that they could be considered by a Strategy Committee consisting of the group leaders of the Lenten discussions. This committee met on May 5 and made a number of recommendations which were forwarded to the next meeting of the Parochial Church Council.

When the council met on May 12, it had these recommendations before it as well as those of the Liturgical Committee's meeting of the previous December; in addition the vicar raised again the question of greater lay participation in the service – the reading of the lessons at matins and evensong, and the reading of the epistle at the communion. He emphasized that such participation would be at his discretion. The council agreed to the proposition about the reading of the lessons but not at that stage to the reading of the epistle by a layman.

The council considered the recommendations of the Liturgical Committee: it declined the suggestion of having more frequent communion services; it preserved the *status quo* about the prayers which were said together; it accepted the suggestion about silence. On the question of what parts should be sung, the council felt that the creed should be said at all times and the gloria sung at all times; the gradual hymn should be retained; the psalms should be said in Lent but sung on other occasions. On almost all matters, the council preferred to continue the current practices.

When faced with the suggestions about worship from the Strategy Committee, the council felt that the appropriate body to consider them would be the Liturgical Committee. A meeting of this group was held on May 14.

The first recommendation was prompted by a concern about a special youth service; rather than that, the Strategy Committee felt that a service on the lines of the People's Service sponsored by the British Broadcasting Corporation should be held monthly with a changing focus on special groups within the community – besides youth, those who had been married in the past five years, and those confirmed in recent years. The idea was accepted, and the first was held on June 6 after an appeal had been sent to those outside the regular congregation by the vicar.

The second group of suggestions was concerned with pursuing further the idea of variety, and two plans emerged. One concerned an interchange of evensong with the neighbouring church at Gopherville. A questionnaire to the members of the congregation at Gopherwood elicited a total agreement to the proposal, and thirty people went to the other church for evensong on May 30; the council at Gopherville agreed to a reciprocal arrangement. A second plan was for a combined service during the summer for all the churches within the group ministry in the area; and the date was fixed for July 25.

The third recommendation concerned the singing or the saying of the psalms; the continuance of the present practice of singing them except in Lent was approved despite some opinions that the psalms should be eliminated altogether. Concerning hymns, the choice was left with the vicar and organist; and some thought was given to the use of *Hymns Ancient and Modern Revised* and the new *Anglican Hymn Book.* On the point of better music and brighter singing, it was agreed that the choir should stay in its usual place and that an attempt should be made to recruit more members. It was felt that some twentieth-century hymn tunes should be used occasionally after suitable practices by the congregation.

The committee also had further thoughts about the resistance of the council to the earlier proposal of some change in the timing and nature of the morning services (Rudge, 1966a, pp. 367–75).

ILLUSTRATIONS OF THE SYSTEMIC THEORY

Z1. You [the bishop of the diocese] have explained the need to set in proper perspective, and enable the clergy and lay people to concentrate upon, the essential aim of the Church, which you quoted to us as 'the spreading of the love of God'.

The Church, then, must become more 'missionary' in its outlook and activities. There is considerable feeling that secondary things have come to the fore, to the detriment of those that are specifically and uniquely Christian. So much of the Church's effort and resources can be, and perhaps have been, devoted to matters of administration, finance, buildings and other areas on the fringes of the Church's life that insufficient attention can be given to more basic spiritual affairs that inadvertently become lost to sight. Yet if the essential aim of the Church is 'the spreading of the love of God', surely even matters of education, social service and morals must all be subordinate to that essential aim. . . .

It is, of course, no part of our responsibility in this review to recommend Church aims or to attach priorities to them. That, the Church must do wholly by itself. We strongly recommend the formation of a Committee on the Church's Mission and Structure to study the aims and priorities of the Church in this Diocese. This Committee would be chaired by you, and might number in its membership the Bishop Suffragan and twelve able clergy and lay people of the Diocese. Counterpart committees should be set up in the parishes.

The Committee on the Church's Mission and Structure should deal not only with aims and priorities but also, once those have been defined, with the organizational structure of the Church to carry them out most effectively. . . .

We recommend that consideration be given to reorganizing the Diocesan structure on the following basis:

(1) Establishing a Diocesan Council, replacing the Executive Committee, to direct and coordinate Diocesan affairs, both spiritual and temporal, and to recommend policy changes to you; composition of the Council should provide appropriate representation of clergy, laymen and lay women, with (i) Synod election from Synod members and others, (ii) appointments by the Archbishop, and (iii) members ex-officio;

(2) Establishing a Committee on Spiritual Affairs, responsible to the Diocesan Council, to coordinate policy on spiritual matters such as the ministry, social service, lay education, missions, publicity and Christian unity, and to advise you and the Bishop Suffragan on these matters;

(3) Establishing a Committee on Administrative Policy and Finance, responsible to the Diocesan Council, to coordinate policy on general administration, finance and property and to watch over the financial affairs of the Diocese;

(4) Establishing, as recommended in section I, a Committee on the Church's Mission and Structure, responsible to the Diocesan Council;

(5) Disbanding the Executive Committee and its sub-committees, which deal mainly with administrative matters;

(6) Disbanding all present committees, boards and councils of Synod;

(7) Establishing a project group to examine the functions and procedures of the Diocesan Synod;

(8) Adding permanent officers to the Diocesan staff and creating numerous boards and project groups leading to the more effective functioning of the Diocese and parishes . . . ;

(9) Making all full-time Diocesan officers responsible to the Bishop Suffragan instead of, as now pertains in some instances, to a council or board . . .

We think it desirable that new areas of work or projects be introduced within this proposed organizational framework, instead of setting up new and parallel structures. It is for this reason that we question the desirability of creating a new World Mission Committee, replete with five sub-committees, at the Diocesan level as has been proposed by

General Synod. By all means, project groups – as many as necessary – can be used, but their activities should be integrated with the work of the permanent officers and boards, and policy aspects handled by the Diocesan Council and its three committees. . . .

We propose that the Diocese add two senior personnel to its permanent staff. One, a Director of Administration, is considered in section IV. The other is an assistant to you and the Bishop Suffragan, perhaps bearing the title of Diocesan Archdeacon . . . He would direct Diocesan activities and coordinate parish activities in spiritual affairs generally, and assist you and the Bishop Suffragan on these affairs in every possible way. He would function as the principal day-to-day liaison officer and channel of communication with the parishes on non-administrative matters, including the dissemination of material developed by boards, project groups and General Synod. He would give especial attention to the fields of lay education, stewardship, lay work, the Rupert's Land News, publicity and evangelism. A Parish Lay Work Advisory Board would work closely with him. . . .

We see a compelling need to appoint a senior Diocesan administrative officer, whom we have titled 'Director of Administration'. Preferably he should be a layman because of the specialized skills required and because the particular qualifications of the clergy can be better used in other areas. He would direct Diocesan activities and coordinate parish activities in administrative affairs generally, including accounting, financial and statistical reports, budgets, finances, office services, purchasing, insurance and property. In the absence of such an officer, a disproportionate part of the time of the Bishop Suffragan has perforce been taken up with administration (Price Waterhouse & Co., 1964, pp. 1, 2–3, 7–8, 9, 12, 14).

Z2. Bishop Chase resigned his see and left the diocese in April 1959; and he was replaced by John Richard Humpidge Moorman who was consecrated on June 11, 1959.

In the early days of his ministry, Bishop Moorman had been in the diocese of Ripon before going on to further parish ministry in other parts of England; and in the years immediately prior to his election he had been principal of a theological college. He achieved a reputation as a scholar, notably in relation to his studies on the life of St Francis.

The general direction of his scholarship was such as to enable him to see clearly the goals and the nature of the church and to be aware of the environment, particularly the ecclesiastical environment, in which the church lived; moreover, his concern for the unity of the church had its counterpart in his conception of the church in systemic terms. Hence, in his address to his first diocesan conference, he said:

> The Church has many problems to face at the present time. It is short of members, short of ministers and short of money. Only about one in every sixteen of the population of adult or adolescent age is an Easter communicant, and perhaps not much more than one in every fifty on an ordinary Sunday. The average number of people which each priest has to care for is now nearly twice what it was when I was a boy, and many of these priests are not as young as they were. For the average age of the clergy is steadily rising, and nearly one-third of the total number are over the age of sixty-five. In a few years' time the number of clergy will almost certainly have sunk even lower than it is now. Of the shortage of money I need hardly speak, as this seems to have been a chronic condition of the Church from apostolic times.
>
> None of these problems can be solved by itself, since each is dependent upon the others. If we had more active members we should have more money and more clergy. If we had more clergy we should almost certainly have more active members and more money. We must therefore try to see the problem as a whole, and not split it up into separate compartments. That is why great efforts in respect of such things as 'recruitment' or 'evangelism' often prove to be so disappointing. It is only when we try to see both the nature and the needs of the Church as a whole that we can begin to plan our work and our policy.
>
> This means that, before all else, we must be clear as to what the Church is, to see it as the body of Christ, the corporative person of the Lord, and, having seen this, to proclaim it by every possible means to the world. We must show men that the work of the Church is not primarily to interest people in religion, nor to provide pious entertainment for those who care for that sort of thing, nor to teach the young to be good citizens, nor to stop people drinking and smoking, nor to balance our parochial and diocesan budgets, nor to do many of the things which absorb so much of our time and energy.
>
> The primary duty of the Church is to be the body on earth of the risen and ascended Christ; to make every man, woman and child understand the loathsomeness of sin – in the world, but more particularly in himself; to bring men face to face with both the goodness and the severity of God; to proclaim the Gospel of man's redemption through the shedding of the Saviour's blood; to strengthen weak and sinful men by administering to them the appointed

means of grace; to be the agents, ambassadors and stewards of a living, loving, active and all-powerful God.

When we learn to do this we shall not have to worry too much about shortages of men, money or ministry, for we shall be doing the Lord's work, and we know that he will not fail his own.

This speech in October 1959 heralded the beginning of a new era.

The image of the diocese was maintained in the ensuing years, not least through the medium of the diocesan publications. The *Gazette* was discontinued at the end of 1958, and in its place was produced a four-page leaflet by a new editor. It retained some of the functions of the former paper in that it included official items such as the appointments of the bishops and moves of the clergy; there was room for a letter from the bishop or a serious article by someone else, but the contributory element that had been so prominent in the *Gazette* in its later phase was dropped. Any spare space was used for notification of events or brief items of comment. It also took a new name: *Ripon Diocesan News*. It was designed for inclusion in parish papers or for circulation by itself; and soon its circulation rose to about 22,000, at which figure it has remained fairly constant.

Although it came into being before the new bishop arrived, it was an appropriate vehicle for his style of leadership: the above quotation filled a page of the issue of November 1959, and similar significant statements followed in other months. He made it an opportunity for the affirmation of the goals of the church: on the appointment of the diocesan missioner, he said, 'Nothing is more important in the work of the Church than evangelism'. He used it to interpet the changing patterns of ministry to the diocese; a full report on the team of specialists was given in January 1965. Many issues were devoted to the changing world environment of which he was very conscious – hence his remark in relation to the place of the laity in church government: 'The Church in a rapidly changing situation needs the best form of government which is possible.'

The main way of interpreting the environment was by straightforward articles by himself, and latterly by others who had special contributions to make, on significant features and events, particularly in the ecclesiastical world. His personal contribution was mainly about the unity of the church, being partly concerned with the Anglican–Methodist conversations and more so with the relations with Rome, especially after his being appointed during 1962 as an official Anglican observer at the Vatican Council. Among the other contributors was a delegate to the Toronto Anglican Congress who wrote about 'Mutual

Responsibility and Interdependence'; another outlined the main theme of the Faith and Order Conference at Nottingham in 1964. The manner of presentation was significant: the facts were given in a lucid way, and it was left for people to respond as they would; occasionally there would be suggestions but not any directions. This was a marked contrast to the situation in the early post-war days when the *Gazette* contained many legal enactments and directions; what environmental factors were introduced then were presented in the form, as in the case of South India, of certain administrative regulations consequent upon the changed situation.

The character of the diocesan conferences showed the same image as the *News*. The standard of the first address was maintained, and the later speeches by the bishop came to be regarded as one of the main features of the proceedings, the attractiveness of which was to a large extent responsible for a rise in attendance from about 300 to a steady level of 400 or so; people felt that it was worth coming to. The bishop thus continued to clarify the goals of the church and to bring the world situation into the diocese. For instance, in June 1963, he took people on 'an imaginary tour of the world, to places of importance in the contemporary ecclesiastical situation': Rome, Istanbul, Toronto, Nottingham, and the Anglican–Methodist conversations. The afternoon sessions of the conference extended these wide interests. By contrast, the formal constitutional and financial business was minimal, except for a major reshuffle of committees which formed the focal point of the reshaping of diocesan life around the new character that was emerging (Rudge, 1966a, pp. 252–7).

Z3. To understand the 'spirit' of First Church, however, we must dig a little deeper. We must go back at least as far as 1950 – a year of discovery and decision for First Church, a year that culminated a long period of soul-searching on the part of the Congregation. The soul-searching had been prompted by the retirement of the distinguished pastor, Dr George W. Allison, and by the prodding questions he asked as his ministry approached its close. Questions like these: Is First Church doing the most it can for the Kingdom of God? Is it using its venerable heritage as the oldest church in the city – or is it resting on the accomplishments of former generations? Is it making the most effective use of its choice location near the heart of the city? Is it adapting to the new opportunities and limitations imposed by a modern city? Is it seeking to claim the city for Christ?

The Congregation became so intrigued with questions like these that it appointed a committee of twelve members to study the mission of

First Church. Granted that the Church is God's servant community, appointed by Him to engage in His work of reconciling the world to Himself, what is His specific assignment to First Church? This committee appointed four sub-committees of twelve members each to ask this question as regards four different aspects of the Church's life. What is the mission of First Church in public worship? In Christian education? In service to the community? In the development of Christian fellowship? These four sub-committees worked for nearly a year and their reports, as coordinated by the original committee and as they have been periodically revised, serve as a kind of charter for the present ministry of First Church.

As a result of this massive effort the Congregation and Session understand the responsibility of First Church in terms of three 'parishes'. One is *the parish of our membership* – we are responsible for nurturing our members in the Christian faith, equipping them for their own ministries as servants of Christ in this world. Another is *the parish of our neighborhood* – we are responsible for showing Christ-like concern for the people who live in the shadow of our building, winning into our Church's reconciling fellowship as many as are led to accept our Lord's invitation. The third is *the parish of our community* – we are responsible for proclaiming God's Word as He speaks to our present human situation, and for becoming involved with whatever enterprises seek to reconcile our city, our nation, and our world to God.

The Session sought to spell out this interpretation of the mission of First Church in more specific terms. Accordingly, in 1950 it adopted the following statement:

'... What is the main business of the Church? A wise man answered this question well when he said that the task of the Church is *to create the creators of a new society*. The business of the Church is to build persons – the kind of persons who in turn will build the Kingdom of God. This means bringing ordinary people under the influence of the personality of Jesus in such a manner that they become extraordinary people – God's people. To accomplish this purpose the Church seeks to impart knowledge and appreciation of the historical facts upon which our faith is founded and to develop a fellowship which will express this new knowledge and appreciation in Christ-like behaviour....'

Our years since 1950 have been mainly spent in implementing the mission of First Church according to this understanding. The implementation has taken three main lines of direction: (1) We have sought to develop a seven-day-a-week program of parish activities which seek to minister to the real-life needs of our parishioners, our neighbors, and our community. (2) We have sought to build a church edifice sufficiently functional to house these activities and sufficiently beautiful to honor our Lord and His Father. (3) We have sought to enlist the services of a professional staff which brings together a group of persons sufficiently skilled to guide our people in their Christian development.

To return to our original question, the most distinctive feature of First Church is probably our sense of mission. We are convinced that God has called us together in this Congregation to serve Him. We know that we serve God and worship Him only as we serve His children. In First Church we believe we have the most effective instrument available to us for this worship and service. . . .

The Staff of First Church is a group of persons who *together* fill the same place in the life of this parish that the pastor fills in the life of a more conventional parish.

Once our Session and Congregation are committed to a seven-day-a-week ministry to our members and through our members to the neighborhood and community, a Staff becomes absolutely necessary. No one person possesses either the energy or the skills required for the professional leadership of such a full-orbed ministry. Only a group of persons with special training and competence in a variety of areas can offer the professional guidance essential for such a ministry. But the group must function as one person, else the program will lack integrity of purpose and expression.

Accordingly, the philosophy undergirding our Staff is expressed by Paul: 'As in one body we have many members, and all the members do not have the same function, so we, though many, are one body in Christ, and individually members one of another' (Romans 12). He was speaking, of course, about the Church, but what he said applies equally well to our Staff. Each Staff member is responsible for such areas of First Church's life as are compatible with his personal competence, training, and concern. At the same time, however, he neither limits himself to those areas for which he is responsible nor isolates himself from the activities for which other Staff members are responsible. While a Staff member is accountable for certain parts of the parish program, he is encouraged to assist other Staff members and to enlist their help. Thus our Staff works together as 'one body'. . . . The Ministry of Parish Mission . . . of Parish Education . . . of Parish Music . . . of Parish Life (First Presbyterian Church, 1963, pp. 17–18, 20–1, 29–31).

Z4. The traditional pattern of ministering was to have one priest in one limited geographical area, and within that area he could reach to people at all points of their lives: within the same boundaries people would be born and die; their children would be brought up and educated there; people would work in that place; in it they would find their leisure; and all the problems of living would be faced within those bounds.

But it is no longer possible to think in terms of one all-embracing geographical area: work, leisure, education, social problems belong to separate areas no longer necessarily related to areas of domicile. Seacroft is no exception – in many ways it is little more than a dormitory.

Nevertheless, the vision behind the creation of Seacroft is that of a new community; and this is at the basis of the new community policy of the church. The ministry of the church must be primarily related to that new community; it must begin at this end, and not be based at the outset on the former conception of a ministry related to domicile.

The most important area of ministry to be developed in the parish of Seacroft is that in relation to the new community – its creation, its right ordering, its redemption. This was the conviction of the former vicar which is shared by the present vicar. The present vicar does have a very considerable ministry in relation to the town centre and with those who are responsible for the destiny of the whole community. The participation in the Seacroft Advisory Group luncheons is one indication of this. The laity of the parish can be of little help at present in that very few of them work in the community or have any positions of responsibility in community affairs. It has also been reported that the laity have no time to engage in this kind of ministry because all their spare time is on 'church' work.

There seems to be a need to rally those who do have some responsibility in community affairs and if necessary free them from ordinary church responsibilities so that they can play their part in this area of ministry. There needs to be some kind of project group of vitally interested and competent people to explore this avenue of ministry further. The vicar is the obvious member of staff to pursue this ministry though others on the staff need not be excluded; and it is important that the vicar be dissociated from any one church – people in the community still think of him as the vicar of St James's, and such association could hinder this ministry if it were felt that it was being undertaken for some ulterior church purpose. It is for this reason that steps should be taken to establish some kind of church centre at the town centre – preferably on an ecumenical basis – and that nothing be done of a permanent nature on the St James's site which will preclude this kind of development.

A ministry is being developed in the parish in respect of those being educated there. A church school is being opened; the vicar has contacts

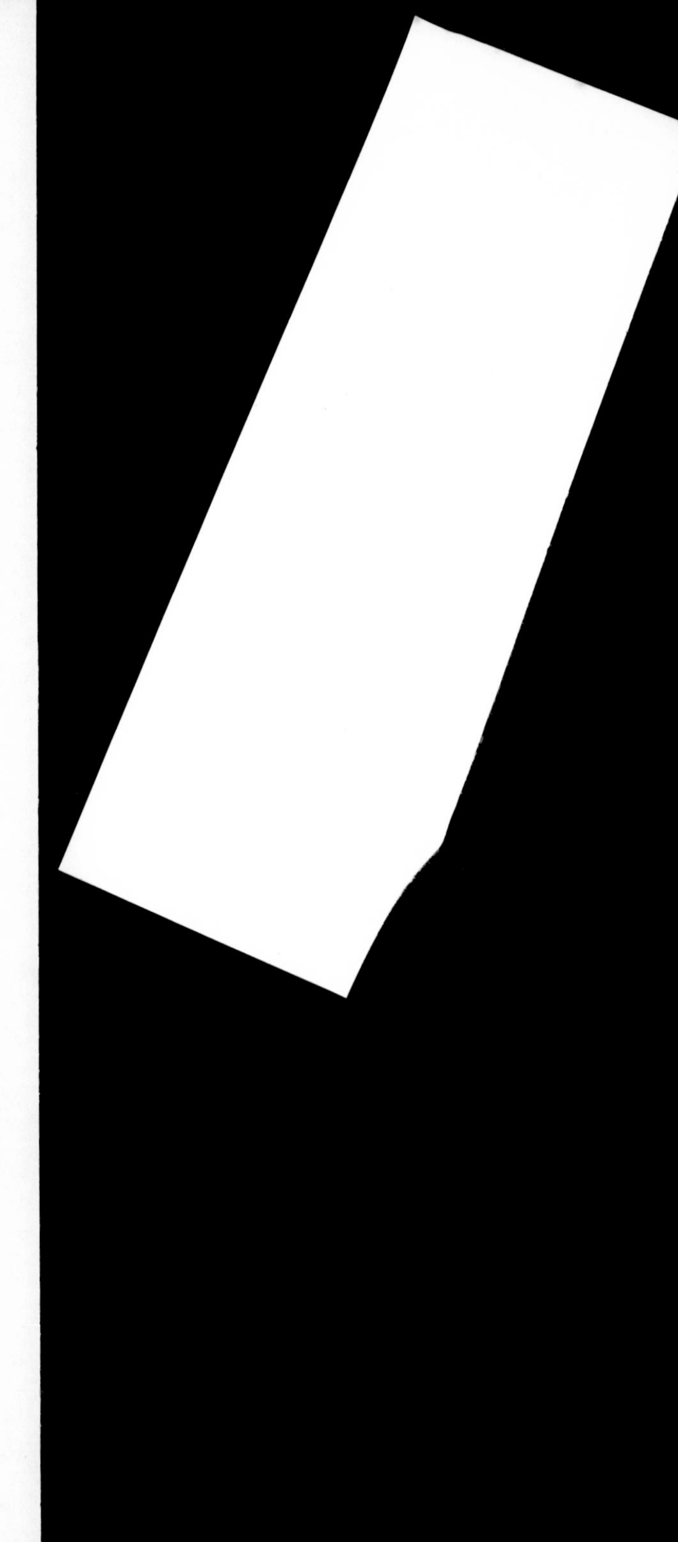

with educational authorities; and two members of the staff teach part-time in schools. Again there is need for a small 'church committee' of expert people to explore and develop this area of ministry.

Two other areas worth exploring are industry and leisure. There may be some scope for the exercise of an industrial chaplaincy; and something is already being done by two members of the staff in the leisure field in respect of music.

These areas of ministry have been placed before the ministry in respect of domicile for several reasons. The present preoccupation with the latter may divert attention away from these fields. The new community policy begins at the new community end, and the resolution of issues at this end may obviate some of the conditions which give rise to those problems which are being met through the present domiciliary ministry – prevention is better than cure. The need for church committees to explore and develop these areas of ministry has important ramifications for the church committees that are related to the domiciliary ministry. It shows that the work of church committees is primarily about ministering and not just about providing, as is the case at present with the existing committees, and that the decision-making in such committees can only be done by experts or by those who are taught to be expert (that is, decisions about ministering can no longer be the expression of 'what we like' but the realization of the will of God in the particular situation in which the church exists) (Rudge, 1966b, pp. 14–16).

CHAPTER 6

Problem Areas in Ecclesiastical Administration

Besides illuminating the general character of church life, the theoretical analysis can serve to clarify and resolve a number of problematic issues in the administrative field. The problems may be found in other organizations, but there are some that are particularly pertinent to the church. They will be discussed in turn: facing a changing world; the nature and extent of a minister's burdens; difficulties resulting from leadership changes or organizational shifts; and the complexity of coexistent power structures. The discussion will include reference to the relevant theory and also illustrations from the previous chapter or from other sources.

FACING A CHANGING WORLD

In all walks of life there is the problem of facing a changing world, a problem all the more acute as the rapidity of change increases; and it may be felt that the difficulty is singularly marked in the life of the church which is so often assumed to be the bastion of unchanging truth and the preserver of an inflexible heritage. The Roman Catholic Church, in particular, is commonly considered as 'not only stubbornly resistant to change, but also as monolithically so' (N. Smelser, in Neal, 1965, Introduction). Yet the church is in the midst of a world of complexity and change; and the rejection of change is but one stance that may be adopted. The question is being wrestled with on many sides. One important study was that of Paul Abrecht, entitled *The Churches and Rapid Social Change* (1961); the Roman Catholic position was the subject of Jeremiah Newman's book *Change and the Catholic Church* (1965).

Besides being concerned with the common topic of facing a changing world, these authors have made valuable contributions by attempting to develop a theoretical treatment of attitudes to change. Abrecht stressed the fluidity of what he called the 'contemporary consultative' type of organization in which the focus is on groups and on the personal relationships within and between them, with the supervisor acting as an integrative agent; by contrast, there is the more rigid form of organization called the 'hierarchical', in which the person in charge is the transmitter of the information to the individuals below him who make up the organization.

Newman's main contrast was between the conservative and liberal attitudes which were clearly evident in the deliberations of the second Vatican Council; in his conclusion, however, he tried to reach a compromise (p. 339):

> If it is a mistake – as it indeed is a mistake – to foster the impression that the 'normal' or 'good' Catholic must necessarily be a conservative, simply speaking, it is equally a mistake that there is no room for conservatism in his make up. We need to get away, once and for all, from such narrow-minded exclusivism and to realize that the Church needs – as we have always needed – both liberals and conservatives, or better, we need conservative liberalism.

These typologies are a precedent for the consideration of the church's attitude to change in terms of the several possible theories of ecclesiastical administration.

The traditional attitude

Those who live according to the traditional theory feel or see innovation in the world around them always in reference to a fixed standard that their organization enshrines: 'things aren't what they used to be'; 'the world is getting worse'. The typical organizational response is the rejection of the external changes and the preservation of the *status quo* in the organization. However, in the church, the questionable point is whether the existing structure is in fact the expression of the gospel or merely the continuation of organizational life appropriate to a bygone age. On the issue of the parson's freehold in the Church of England, it is argued that this is essential to a prophetic ministry in that it enables a minister to preach without fear or favour; but in fact the particular character of the freehold is a personnel policy related to a feudal community. Another difficulty is that the church that adopts the traditional stance gathers around it other forces of conservatism which have no necessary connection with the purpose of the church. The influence of people who are concerned with the preservation of ancient buildings is very noticeable in the Church of England; and in newer countries such as Canada and Australia, the Anglican Church can be the rallying-point for those whose interests are primarily patriotic or linguistic, as if the gospel were dependent on being expressed in Elizabethan English.

Nevertheless, a more positive response than rejection is possible within the terms of the traditional theory. Where the change is imperceptible or only gradual, an organization can respond by dealing with each point of innovation as it arises; without making any fundamental alteration in the main body, a new structure can be added to develop a new piece of work. This is the way in which missionary societies grew in the Church of England. The demands for self-government in that church (C1, p. 79) were met by adding the new machinery of the Church Assembly (X1, p. 85) to the existing governing bodies of the convocations. The pre-war structure of the diocese of Ripon (A3, p. 73) developed in this way; so did the central machinery of the Church of England in spite of its intended classical shape. By the 1950s, there were some twenty-two bodies attached in various ways to the Church Assembly. The piecemeal approach can thus lead to such complexity of organization that a major reorganization may be necessary to clear away the encumbrances; and the fear of this can strengthen the original desire to reject change altogether.

The charismatic stance

The charismatic theory is an approach to organizational life that is basically geared to a world of change and upheaval. The changes are sensed intuitively by the charismatic leader who is able to crystallize action around an entirely new focus of life based on his notions or revelations. An entirely new organization is the result and it is held together by the magnetic force of his personality. Bishop Burroughs (C2, p. 82) was of this character, but there was a haphazard element in his way of operating that made it difficult to follow; Archbishop Temple's manner of action (C1, p. 79), even in his archiepiscopal days, led to many uncertainties.

However, a charismatic leader can articulate the forces of social change in such a way as to give some clarity and security of purpose in a time of upheaval or in a novel environment. The result of a parish mission in a certain new housing area was the permanent reshaping of parish life – hitherto run on traditional lines – in relation to the emerging new sociological character: groups were formed of people who lived in the same or neighbouring streets; the services were changed to allow for more family attendance and for participation by children; a very readable broadsheet replaced a somewhat solemn old-style parish paper. These things sprang out of the missioner's perception of the situation, whereas, before, the new social factors had been either ignored or not even recognized. Nevertheless, a charismatic approach cannot be taken up at will; nobody can consciously choose to adopt this theory to cope with change; it is but the means of understanding what happens when a person of this type appears.

The classical theory

In the terms of the classical theory, the changing world is known through careful investigation and study; and this information is given to the planners who then produce a scheme to take account of the new situation. But a fundamental weakness springs from the fact that one department does the investigating and another does the planning; the operation is a series of discrete steps; and the outcome can be out of touch with the realities. How many buildings, be they bridges or hospitals or churches, are found to be too small or in need of modification even before they are completed! Change is a continuous process; whereas the administrative process is a series of discrete steps whose validity depends on the assumption that the world will stay still while the plans are made. The organization can deal with change only on its own terms; in fact, the theory is designed to cope not with change but with mass, homogeneous conditions that are essentially stable. Yet this theory has been adopted extensively in the church: much of the pastoral reorganization in the Church of England has been in these terms. In a certain diocese (X6, p. 88), a comprehensive, step-by-step programme was implemented; but to some extent it was accompanied by the assumption that this would be a once-for-all reorganization whereas, on the completion of the scheme, there was need for further continuing work in this area to keep pace with new conditions.

The human relations approach

The human relations approach to the issue of change is that the variations in the external world are felt and known through their impact on the members of the organization; such features are brought out into the open in group discussion or through non-directive counselling. The objective of the organization then becomes helping its members to cope with problems caused by the pressure of events on them. Thus, in a central city church, a ministry was extended towards all kinds of people in need who came to it. There were alcoholics, there were lonely people, there were people who could not adjust to life in new housing areas and who could not feel at home in the churches there; and in the light of such needs a considerable counselling ministry was developed together with group activities which had a therapeutic value – but the essence of the work was that it was dealing with effects and not with causes. This approach can lead to an attitude of acquiescence towards the changing external situation and to a concentration of effort on ameliorating its consequences (Y2, p. 95).

The group approach can bring an element of variability into an organization that would seemingly fit the organization for its role in a fluid environment; but the theory provides no guidelines for the management of variables – there is no serious focus on the purpose of the organization or on the nature of the external world, as was evident in the case of the proposed liturgical changes (Y3, p. 97). Techniques of planned change have been developed to facilitate organizational shifts – such a passage may be smoother and more acceptable than the classical imposition of a plan – but they are of limited use if the plans are conceived in the same discrete terms as in the classical theory. In a kaleidoscopic world, the problem is not so much 'planned change' as 'changed plans'.

The systemic position

It is on this latter point that the systemic theory makes its major contribution in relation to change. Plans are not fixed things that unfortunately have to be changed: the essence of this theory is that there is provision for continuous adaptation. The changes are investigated in the same thorough way as envisaged in the classical theory, but there is a continuous process of interpreting the changes to the whole organization so that action can be taken where initiative is needed; and the whole organization is reshaped around this new emphasis (not newly created, as in the terms of the charismatic theory). The response is thus by the whole system (not by one department) because the whole body takes its shape from the two definitive items of purpose and situation. The organization is designed to fit the world around it rather than vice versa as in the classical theory; and the rapport with the environment – fundamental to the traditional theory – is maintained even though that environment is continually on the move.

A restructuring of a church on these lines was envisaged in the consultation on organization in the Anglican Church of Canada in 1965. The general perspective was expressed in the preamble (p. 400):

> For thousands of years Man has been able to survive because of his ability to adjust to changing circumstances and changing environment. On the other hand the Dinosaur is extinct because it put its faith in protective bone tissue and a defensive apparatus that was rigid and inflexible. *We do not advocate change for the sake of change. We see change as the condition of survival.*

The committee then designed a structure on the lines of the systemic theory: noteworthy was its emphasis on the unity of the church's mission and the need for great flexibility. An officer in charge of the newly created Office of Program Planning and Research would be the focal point in the process of continuing adaptation because, the committee said (p. 405), 'there needs to be an over-all view of the Church's work and mission so that the Church's "program" can reflect as quickly as possible and as profoundly as possible the Church's fundamental tasks in a particular period'. The concept of a programme was thus not a discrete plan but a continuous concern for the fulfilling of the church's purpose in the midst of a very fluid situation.

The pressure of change in the world around – which prompted this review of the structure of the Anglican Church in Canada – has had a considerable impact on almost all churches; and many have sought to respond. In some the church leaders have thought profoundly about how to adapt to a changing world, as did the Canadian officers. Other churches have engaged consultants to help them with the problem, and the reports produced by them have had a considerable similarity with the proposals of the systemic theory; in the diocese of Rupert's Land (Z1, p. 102), the Committee on the Church's Mission and Structure would act as the monitoring agent in adapting the whole diocese to new perspectives. Some churches have struggled on as best they could, realizing that the new environment called for measures unprecedented in any known pattern of operation. Various scholars, faced with the ferment in the church and the complexity of the world around, have attempted organizational diagnoses and prescriptions. In America, Harvey Cox produced a noteworthy book entitled *The Secular City* (1965), in which he forecast the characteristics of future church organization: flexible, future-oriented, secularized, and with a limited claim on its members. In another passage he said (p. 157), 'We will need a widely differentiated range of different types of church organization'; he was also concerned with the theological dimension (p. 105): 'The starting-point for any theology of the church today must be a theology of social change.' The similar movement in England, often called 'The New Theology', has prompted some thinking on church organization: J. A. T. Robinson included a section in his book *The New Reformation?* (1965, pp. 88–100), and there have been discussions in periodicals such as *Prism* and *Parish and People*. In addition, there has been a considerable amount of research, particularly in Western Europe, under the auspices of the World Council of Churches, notably on the topic of 'the missionary structure of the congregation'.

All this ferment of thinking about the organizational response of the church to a changing world may be disturbing to those who adopt the normal American approach to ecclesiastical administration, and more so to those in the English tradition. Yet the great virtue of the systemic theory (to which many of the new ideas correspond) is that it can give substance and integrity to the kinds of thinking and ways of operating to which people have been almost driven in the face of the world of change around them. The theory gives both theological and managerial soundness to the church, which is itself in as great a state of flux as is the environment in which it exists.

THE NATURE AND EXTENT OF A MINISTER'S BURDENS

The ministry of the church is not exempt from one of the problems common to many areas of life, namely, the pressure of work on those who hold executive positions. Such intensity can result in overwork, ulcers, nervous breakdown, premature retirement, even heart attacks and death.

Those who have observed the life of ministers have noted similar pressures and similar results. Perhaps a sign of the times was the publication in 1965 of a book called *Psychological Studies of Clergymen*

(Menges and Dittes), which was a lengthy collection of abstracts of all that has been written hitherto on this subject. Many sociologists of religion have examined the issue in detail. In his survey of urban ministers in the United States, Samuel W. Blizzard (1956, p. 35) found that the average minister spent 38 per cent of his time as an administrator and 12 per cent as an organizer. Similar figures were produced by Moberg (1962, p. 497), who felt that the proportion of time so spent was increasing. In investigating the English scene, Paul (1964, p. 74) found that there was a correlation between the pressure of administrative work and the density of the population; that is, those clergy who were engaged in highly urbanized areas were being burdened with increasing amounts of administration. A further indication of the widespread nature of the problem was the study by Richard H. T. Thompson (1957, p. 11) in New Zealand, who observed that, although his figures showed a smaller proportion of time spent on administration than did the American studies, 'it should be borne in mind that . . . administrative and other activities though individually small may nevertheless collectively take up large amounts of time'. Besides the actual burden of work in terms of time and effort, there is often an accompanying sense of irritation and frustration – the above writers gave evidence of this – and this can lead to more serious psychological and nervous troubles. It would be interesting to know how many men were lost to the active ministry because of these circumstances.

On this general issue, the study of ecclesiastical administration is particularly pertinent. The nature and extent of the involvement of the minister depend on which theory of ecclesiastical administration he follows.

Running a machine

The point can be seen most clearly by reference to the classical theory. The essence of this theory is that the leader sees his work as running a machine: he has to make it go, he provides the initiative, he issues the orders, he specifies every detail of procedure, he makes each part move in its appointed way, and he checks on performance. His task, then, requires a great expenditure of energy and a considerable involvement in detail. Such a situation may arise when a minister sets out with the classical approach in mind. The new incumbent (X7, p. 89) had a lot of ideas about how he was going to run his parish; he took action on many fronts; but by the end of the second month, he was feeling the pressure of all the details of a very busy programme.

A more difficult situation arises when a church leader is appointed to a post in a church which is structured on classical lines; he becomes involved in the fulfilling of his office even though he does not choose to follow a classical path himself. Harrison (1959) showed how the structure of the American Baptist Convention was developed on the lines of the classical theory and how those who held senior posts were virtually forced into working in that pattern; so much so that even men with extreme views could be placed in such positions because the very pressures of the organization would neutralize any wayward tendencies. A similar situation prevails to some extent in the Church of England, where much of the superstructure is on classical lines; bishops and archbishops whose background is generally in the traditional theory are virtually required to become administrators; and the circumstances of office are such as to subdue the outspokenness of some who have been raised to the episcopate. Some, however, have had a flair for administration; Archbishop Fisher, rightly or wrongly, has been described as in this category. He could handle the role required of him; but his fellow archbishop at York noted that 'he was inclined both from the Chair and behind the scenes to interfere too much in detail as well as in policy' (Smyth, 1959, p. 341).

The consequence of operating in the classical manner is involvement in administrative detail; not just involvement, but an increasing entanglement. Ultimately it is not the leader who runs the machine; it is the machine that runs him. The faster he is able to make it go, the more he becomes its victim (e.g. X7, p. 89).

In order to modify this inherent feature of a classical type of organization, certain restraining devices have been developed. One is called 'the span of control'. The span refers to the number of people who are supervised by a leader, that is, the number of posts immediately related to his on the next line of the organization chart. Management theorists have shown that, as this number grows arithmetically, the number of relationships that the manager has to consider grows geometrically. This multiplication means that the limit to the number of subordinates that one person can effectively supervise is quickly reached: the figure is sometimes put at about five or six. The fixing of such a maximum is in fact an attempt to keep an executive's work within manageable limits; presumably a similar kind of limit applies to ministers.

Another device is known as delegation. This is based on the classical assumption that all work in the organization belongs to the manager, depending as it does on his initiative and drive. As the work grows beyond the capacity of one man, so he allots certain jobs to his subordinates; but the work still remains his – he decides what is done, and how and when it is done, and he has to check on his juniors' performance to see that they have carried out his instructions. Delegation is thus only a partial answer to the administrative burdens of a manager who operates in terms of the classical theory.

There are special problems about delegation in organizations such as churches which, especially on the local level, rely considerably on voluntary help. Volunteers may not be fully competent and so may require more than usual supervision. Their terms of service make it difficult to insist on deadlines, with the result that it may often be more satisfactory for the minister to do the job himself; he may spend more time and effort in finding the right person at the right time than he would use in performing the task himself.

There are difficulties, then, in trying to apply these restraining devices to the multiplication of administrative burdens; the more adequate solution may be to find an alternative manner of operating which does not have such responsibilities as its normal concomitant.

Consequences of charismatic leadership

The leader who follows the charismatic pattern is involved in anything and everything that is related to the pursuance of his particular cause or vision or intuition. The intensity of his involvement may be even greater than that of a classical type of leader, owing to the high degree of commitment that is essential in a charismatic leader and the great extent to which he depends on the success of his venture – he must do everything possible to see that he does not fail, nor lose the support of those who have been won to his cause.

Such a commitment precludes the adoption of such classical devices as the span of control: there can be no mechanistic limit to involvement; to suggest that there was would be to deny the essential compelling quality of the vision. Moreover, there is no room for delegation: the work is so personally related to the one leader that he would find it hard to put it into the hands of others; also his ways are likely to be so random as to make it impossible for another person to render much assistance.

The burdens of this type of leadership are well illustrated in the life of Bishop Burroughs (C2, p. 82), and notably in the life of Archbishop William Temple, whose premature decease prompted his biographer (Iremonger, 1948) to write in trenchant terms. After noting (p. viii) that 'he flung himself with unsparing, and at times reckless, vigour into the active pursuit of his (and his friends') ideals', Iremonger went on (p. xi):

> But there is a warning, and we must not neglect it. Apart from his share in the high affairs of State, the Archbishop of Canterbury has to carry a crushing burden of administration and of sheer relentless routine work of which the public has simply no idea. He has nothing like an adequate secretariat and is asked to do the work of a Prime Minister with the apparatus of a headmaster. At the time of Dr Temple's translation fears were felt that he might be overwhelmed by it, and find himself unable to continue what he had hitherto done so brilliantly. He refused to allow that to happen. He was everywhere, unspared and unsparing, constantly travelling up and down the country under the trying conditions of war-time, addressing audiences of every kind and touching the life of the nation at every point. He still persisted in putting into practice his own interpretation of his office and of national religious leadership. He did this not by shirking or neglecting the unrespiting official work of Lambeth – which is in itself more than a man can carry – or the pastoral care of his diocese, but by attempting to do this all at once. It killed him. Is the Church so rich in prophets that it can afford to squander the gifts of God? This lesson must be laid to heart. Some rearrangement has become imperative.

Iremonger campaigned for the establishment of a general headquarters for the Church of England; he felt that such an organization would relieve the burdens of responsibility on the archbishop – but the question remains whether a charismatic type of leader would use, or could use, such an office.

Another important aspect of charismatic leadership is revealed in the case of a parish priest who somewhat intuitively chose at the beginning of his incumbency to preserve a church school in his parish as a government-aided rather than a government-controlled school. The project involved the raising of a considerable sum of money to finance the venture; but he set about organizing a general appeal with much enthusiasm. He enlisted the support of surrounding parishes and rural deaneries; and eventually called a public meeting under the patronage of the local mayor. The outcome was the formation of a committee of which the vicar was appointed chairman. There was a burst of activity in the first twelve months with frequent meetings of the committee and its executive with a view to launching a drive for funds. Money was attracted to the cause and the prospects seemed rosy; but there was a hitch in the arrangements about the site for the new building, and the construction had to be delayed. The postponement of the 'messianic event' dampened the enthusiasm of potential subscribers; it also weakened the morale of the members of the committee. Several years elapsed until hopes were revived once more by successful negotiations about the site, and further attempts were made to appeal to people's generosity; but virtually nothing came of the renewed effort. The financial burden was increased by the enlargement of the scheme to include a neighbouring parish school, and this seemed to make the situation more hopeless. In the meantime, the size of the committee dwindled through the departure of some members from the town and the loss of interest by others; it was reduced to its executive and eventually to one person – the vicar who started the idea. He had been immersed in the project in its heyday; great demands were made on him then, but his burdens were in fact increased when the charisma began to wane. He lost the assistance of his supporters and was left to carry the responsibility alone; and he felt obliged to do this because his reputation was dependent on the success of the whole enterprise which sprang originally from his intuitive decision.

If the charismatic element is regarded as an essential element in the ministry, it is easy to see how the administrative burdens of ministers become intolerable and lead to breakdowns.

The traditional position

One of the factors that shape the picture in the traditional theory is that the leader is in a paternal position (e.g. A3, p. 73): all parts of the organization look to him not for drive but for patronage; he has to attend and give his blessing to all that takes place; some functions may be interesting but others may be dull, boring, and prolonged. He is expected to perform all the ancient rituals that hallow the life of the organization; but outworn customs and outdated ceremonies can be very wearisome. Yet he dare not withdraw from such activities.

It has been noted how the slow process of adjustment to change can lead to a very cumbersome form of organization: all parts require the attention of the leader to the point of occupying all his time and energy. Many bishops and clergy in the Church of England, for instance, have the dual responsibility of attending meetings of the Church Assembly and its committees along with meetings of the convocations. Perhaps it was the statesmanlike qualities of Archbishop Davidson (A1, p. 71) that shielded him from the burdens and frustrations that can accompany the traditional type of leadership; but his less detached successor (A2, p. 72) complained of the excessive burdens as being 'incredible, indefensible, and inevitable' (Lockhart, 1949, p. 372).

A great difficulty for many English clergy is the carry-over of a way of life from the days when there were servants and maids to perform many of the menial duties in the vicarage or church. Nowadays many clergy are virtually in a servile position, being occupied to no small extent in such jobs as stoking the heater in the residence or the church and cleaning the church hall or school (as noted in A4, p. 78, and X7, p. 89).

Another basic difficulty is the fusion of private and public life implicit in this approach. Even the home cannot be a refuge from all the demands of a parish: the wife can be the slave of the telephone or the door-bell; and the privacy of the home can be invaded by parishioners as if it were their right.

Is there freedom in the human relations approach?

It may be felt that the way to escape the extensive and frustrating burdens of office is for a minister to spend his time with people, so that he can perform the ministry for which he was really ordained. The human relations approach with its personal emphasis may therefore seem an attractive solution.

Nevertheless this is a false expectation. There is a limit to the number of clients that a professional counsellor is able to see; any attempt to extend such work beyond this form of 'span of control' will lead to great demands on the physical and spiritual resources of a man. Yet there is always the temptation to do more; and the more a minister is known for doing the work well, the greater will be the number of claimants on his time. Moreover, ministers may not have the professional detachment to limit their load in this way.

Parochial policies which spring from this approach can make great demands on a minister's resources. To keep a large number of discussion groups going can be exhausting; in a parish where there were many house church meetings, the few clergy were hard pressed to keep in touch with them all and yet the scheme depended on their presence; the vicar at Gopherwood (Y3, p. 97) found himself greatly entangled in all the complicated negotiations about liturgical reform.

Further, the personal approach can often touch on intense emotional and psychological difficulties and this may be done unnecessarily. Once a very respected priest was brought into a group-life laboratory; the experience aroused some peculiar personal problems in the group; and this priest was so emotionally upset that the leader had to spend most of the next week dealing with the disturbance that had been so needlessly brought about.

Moreover, the group approach can lead to inflated ideas of importance in the leader: he may gain great personal satisfaction out of his counselling to the point of retaining clients rather than healing them. Further, his prepossession with problems may distract him from seeing how they may be dealt with at the source; and so the same clients come again and again to receive help in respect of issues that are really consequential. The false sense of satisfaction about working with personal problems may well give the leader a false sense of what is the real extent of his burdens.

None of these kinds of involvement may be inherent in, or intended in, the human relations approach; but such leadership can degenerate in these ways – there is no clear safeguard against these untoward developments.

The systemic solution

The way in which the burdens of office are relieved according to the systemic theory lies in the fact that there is no mechanistic nexus between the actions of the leader and the activities of the enterprise, as there is in the classical theory. The function of the leader is to monitor the organization, not to run it or drive it. He gives the perspective, not the orders; and the control is not through close supervision in relation to regulations but by reference to the purpose of the whole body to which the members are committed. There is no mechanistic limit to the size of the system that one person may monitor; an increase in size does not necessarily mean an increase in the load that he carries.

There is no need to resort to delegation because the work of the organization belongs to the whole system, not to one man; the initiative is taken by those who are competent at the point at which action is needed; and the administrative work (in the narrow sense) is recognized for what it is and is provided for in the maintaining function of the organization, to which responsible people are appointed. The extent of such administrative work is also lessened: there is not the dependence on the file as in the classical theory; there is less need for records and paperwork because the situation is so fluid that the value of many documents passes as soon as they have been used; nor has the organization any particular interest in collecting documents for the sake of having the tradition preserved.

In the diocese of Rupert's Land (Z1, p. 102), the idea behind the appointments of a diocesan archdeacon for the supervision of the ministering work and of a director of administration in charge of the maintaining function was to release the bishop and his assistant from their involvement in detail, particularly in the latter area. Bishop Moorman (Z2, p. 104) was sufficiently detached from urgent business in his diocese to be able to spend considerable periods as the chief Anglican observer at the second Vatican Council; and such outside contacts, rather than hindering his leadership in the diocese, meant that he was able to widen the horizons of diocesan life and stimulate new interest. A somewhat novel illustration is that of a priest who took charge of a parish during an extended interregnum; his terms were that he could be there only on the Sundays. He was not engaged in anything at all during the week; and even on Sundays his responsibilities did not go much beyond conducting the services and preaching because of the way in which the churchwardens, verger, and laity carried out their duties. Through his preaching, the priest was able to bring a fresh vision to the congregation; and the outcome was that, even after an interval of nine months, church life was still strong. Many of the people welcomed the opportunity to respond, particularly after a somewhat authoritarian régime in the past.

The freedom from involvement, given in the terms of reference in this last case, can be the result of deliberate choice should a minister follow the pattern of the systemic theory. In addition to this freedom, the minister has the satisfaction of fulfilling his real ministry: the monitoring function is the organizational expression of the cherished roles of prophet, priest, and pastor.

CHANGES IN ORGANIZATIONAL PATTERNS

One of the problems in the church is that of alterations in organizational life consequent upon a change in leadership or the adoption of some new policy. This issue is not limited to ecclesiastical bodies; it is experienced in all kinds of organizations. One example that has been investigated academically was that of a change in the ownership of a gypsum plant in the United States, which was the basis of Alvin W. Gouldner's book *Patterns of Industrial Bureaucracy* (1954).

Problems deriving from leadership changes have always been present in churches, although they have often been dismissed as being somewhat unimportant: 'Each man has his own way of working and needs to arrange things to suit himself', it is sometimes said. Another view is that in the providence of God the contribution of one leader complements that of another: in a parish of ancient origin, there was a parish priest who spent fifty years in the parish; he was a great pastor who ministered to his people but he did not do much about the property of the church; his successor, in contrast, was assiduous in his concern for the fabric of the church properties but left the pastoral care of the people mainly to a curate while he himself was an absentee – a comment was, 'taking the long view, each complemented the other'.

An alternative to dismissing the issue is to minimize the problems involved by adopting an appropriate personnel policy in the areas of training or selection. The effects of diversity of character may be reduced through the kind of training given, for instance, in Roman Catholic seminaries or in the diocesan colleges of the Church of England in Australia. Appointments have been restricted to men of one particular churchmanship through the operation of patronage trusts in England, through the development of dioceses of a monochrome character, and through consistency in the character of a local church which has the right of appointing its minister. Such personnel devices serve to limit the extent of the problems consequent upon leadership changes.

However, the issue still remains and it is of real importance to both minister and laity; it can give rise to difficulties, tensions, quarrels, and conflicts. These phenomena, though manifest in personal relationships between the leader and the led, are basically organizational in origin. The value of the theory of ecclesiastical administration is that it can serve as the tool for the analysis of such matters; and by means of it, the problems can be understood and even anticipated. The problems are real because an organizational change is not mechanistic like the flicking of a switch: it impinges on people and on their desires and feelings; it encounters the persistence of hopes and expectations; it touches on established practices and accepted ways of operating; it can become embodied in physical terms in the form of buildings and other fixed items. This last point is dealt with more fully in the discussion of building policy; at this stage, attention is given mainly to the two sides of the compliance relationship.

The number of possible organizational changes is twenty, that is, the number of permutations of two theories of ecclesiastical administration from five; but it is convenient to group together those changes that do not include the systemic theory and those that do. The reason behind this distinction is that it is assumed that the first four theories will still have some adherents; and it is important to understand the problems that are involved in changing from one of these four to another. The second area of consideration is that of the issues involved in moving to the chosen systemic pattern of operation and in falling away from it.

CHANGES NOT INCLUDING THE SYSTEMIC THEORY

Traditional to charismatic and vice versa

In the exposition of the first two theories, note was made of their antithetical stance, and this is the key to what happens when a charismatic type of leader follows a traditional type, or inherits a situation shaped on the lines of the traditional theory. There is likely to be disruption and antagonism. Those who follow the former pattern of life will be upset by the vigour, the outspokenness, the randomness of action on the part of the new leader; and he will always be fighting against the rearguard action of the members in the organization. People who do not see the impelling character of the new vision will feel left out: in a certain parish (C3, p. 82), a new vicar galvanized the church into action through the introduction of the parish communion and the westward position of the celebrant; around this new concept of life were gathered new organizations such as a young women's group and the youth club; but the existing parish bodies which had their own charters in their respective national organizations – scouts, guides, Girls' Friendly Society – were left out on their own and they withered for lack of care and for loss of the sense of belonging to which they had been accustomed.

At other times, charismatic leadership can give new life to a church that has become moribund or run down. In such circumstances, it is common for the personnel policy to be: 'Send in a dynamic character who can really get things moving!' Such a person can stir a church out of the doldrums that have developed through the pursuance of the traditional theory. In this way, Archbishop Temple brought new vision and vigour to the Church of England after the somewhat uninspired leadership of Archbishop Lang; and the vicar of Hollywood brought life to a situation described as 'disconsolate' (C3, p. 82). Another contribution of a charismatic type of leader can be to articulate the forces of social change in such a way as to transform the life of the church, as in the case of the parish mission whereby the impact of the missioner was such as to reshape the traditionally oriented parish to meet the needs of people living in the new environment of a housing estate.

The reverse movement has important consequences, too. For a traditional type of leader to take over an organization that has been focused on a magnetic personality would be disastrous for it: all its vigour, its enthusiasm, its vision would be destroyed. Archbishop Davidson (A1, p. 71), for instance, did all he could to dismiss the pressures arising from the Life and Liberty Movement in the Church of England (C1, p. 79); he tried to dampen the enthusiasm of its members and to curb its potentially explosive content.

Traditional to classical and vice versa

The transition from the traditional to the classical is one of the fundamental shifts in organizational life and it stirs the deepest emotions besides creating the most complex problems. There is a deeply rooted fear in the English tradition of ecclesiastical administration of anything that savours of the classical theory. When the Ridley report (1956) on reorganization on the national level was introduced into the Church Assembly, it was branded as 'over-organizing', 'streamlining', 'rationalizing', even as 'Americanization', though in fact the report was not couched in terms of the classical theory at all. There was alarm at the possibility of the direction of clergy at the behest of regional patronage boards as proposed in the Paul report (1964). Bishop Lunt (A3, p. 73) looked with dismay on the proposals for reorganization in the church that were mooted in the later war period in his diocese (X3, p. 86, X4, p. 87); and the parishioners in the case where the new incumbent tried to run the parish as a machine (X7, p. 89) resisted his demands by saying that they did not want anything too religious. At the same time, a classical type of leader would be puzzled at the inability of people 'to see reason' and he would feel thwarted by their unwillingness to join in his schemes.

The reverse process is the commonest cause of role conflict that clergy experience. They come to an organization that is shaped on classical lines; it is required of them that they be administrators and organizers; but they feel that such an emphasis is the denial of the ministry to which they have been ordained. They are caught in a dilemma: if they lead in a classical way, they feel frustrated in their ministry; if they do not lead in this way, the organization comes to a halt for want of drive on their part. For instance, a certain parish was in process of creation; but the development was seen in terms of achieving a certain number of quantitative objectives – the drawing of certain boundaries, the accumulation of funds, the erection of specified buildings, the publishing of a magazine, the appointment of staff – and all these items demanded the attention of the priest-in-charge; he felt that these preoccupations were a denial of his real ministry to people, yet he could not fail to attend to all of them lest the parish never become viable.

Traditional to human relations and vice versa

The difficulty about shifting from a traditional to a human relations position is that the latter requires a degree of sophistication and conscious participation that is beyond the reach of the type of person characteristic of the traditional theory. The human relations approach may appeal only to a small number; group dynamics may be engrossing for the esoteric few, but a complete mystery to the rest. Deep down there is a fear that all the techniques of group activities are but a subtle means of manipulation and are no more acceptable than the directive element of the classical theory. In a rural parish, the vicar engaged a human relations type of leader to conduct a quiet afternoon for his parishioners; but the only people who came were those who had had some previous experience in group activities and they were introduced to a way of parish life that would be entirely foreign to the remainder of the parishioners. Another vicar gathered a group of people around him with a view to undertaking intensive pastoral care of the sick, the aged, and problem families; the group members became very enthusiastic about their work, but their exuberance was soon dampened by the unwillingness of the parishioners to appreciate their attention: they preferred the old-fashioned ministry of the vicar. In a further case (Y3, p. 97), the vicar embarked on a programme of liturgical inquiry in a small country parish; he was abetted by a small group of sophisticated people who produced all kinds of bright ideas; but the programme was meaningless to the ordinary country people, who resisted the changes at almost every point – and the minister was frustrated by their apparent insensitivity.

The reverse position is where a traditional type of leader takes over a situation that has been shaped extensively in terms of group activity. The leader would be confused by the many voices of those who wished to participate; and these people would feel thwarted by the new minister's not allowing their contributions to be heard and used.

Charismatic to classical and vice versa

The transition from the charismatic to the classical was described as a process of 'routinization' by Weber (1947). The adoption of the classical approach in such a context would mean regularizing what had been hitherto somewhat random and putting on a permanent, organized basis what had previously depended on the dynamic character of one person. Such a process can lead to a loss of the vision that inspired the earlier movement. In the creation of a new parish there was a considerable amount of initial enthusiasm, but when the task became a reality, and especially when it was divided into a series of proximate ends such as providing essential buildings or funds, the glamour disappeared and the people were left with an uninspiring, uphill battle to achieve their goals. A notable instance of the process was the transformation of the Life and Liberty Movement in the Church of England into constitutional form under the Enabling Act (X1, p. 85). Very soon the distinction was made between the spiritual and the material, with the machinery of church government being left with the latter; the fire of the original movement was quenched; although much useful work was done, the progress was somewhat pedestrian; and charges of bureaucratic development were soon heard (X2, p. 86).

Conversely, the change to a charismatic approach can lead to great uncertainty in an organization run on classical lines: those in official positions would be at a loss as to what to do in the face of the apparent random activities of a new charismatic leader. Yet such a leader can help to restore the vision and dynamism that can be lost in a classical type of organization; but this is in fact the essence of sectarian tendencies – the attempt to revive the original purity of the revelation.

Charismatic to human relations and vice versa

The step from a charismatic posture to a human relations one is comparatively smooth: both approaches depend on active participation and response, the former being intuitive, the latter being just as spontaneous but more conscious and intelligent; but the people involved may well miss the dynamic quality of the charismatic leader and feel somewhat at a loss for a focus for their activities.

In the reverse process, people who are accustomed to a human relations approach might welcome a clearer perspective on the purpose of the organization but resent the disparagement of the intellect that is implicit in the expectation of an intuitive response.

Classical to human relations and vice versa

Should a human relations type of leader take over a church run on classical principles, he would feel thwarted by the expectation that he should be an organizer and administrator – somewhat on the same lines as the role conflict experienced by a traditional type of minister. Those in the organization might feel that the new approach would lead to uncertainty of direction and maybe to anarchy. A bishop (Y1, p. 94) whose episcopate was dominated in the early part by the classical character of the diocese (X5, p. 88) eventually managed to bring his democratic emphasis to the fore, but in many areas of diocesan life there was uncertainty as to the way to go; people were not used to making, or able to make, the necessary decisions themselves. Yet it could be imagined that in some circumstances people would welcome the room for freedom and initiative that would follow from the human relations approach.

On the other hand, those who had become accustomed to operating in this way would feel frustrated by the demands and directions of a classical leader; they would resent the rigidity of organization imposed on their very fluid relationships. Nevertheless, should the human relations approach lead to anarchy, then the classical kind of leadership would have the effect of restoring some sense of order and purpose to the situation.

CHANGES INCLUDING THE SYSTEMIC THEORY

The second series of organizational changes are those that involve the systemic theory. Should this theory be adopted in the light of its theological foundations, it is useful to know how it can be grafted onto an organization that is shaped in terms of one or other of the theories. There are important points of difference between the systemic and the other points of view; but there are also significant similarities, and these should be stressed so as to show the essential continuity of approach.

Traditional to systemic

The systemic and the traditional theories seem poles apart in that one is related to a static environment, the other to a rapidly changing and complex situation; yet they have the common systemic conception of an organization though it is less apparent in the traditional position, and in both theories a complete rapport with the world around is envisaged. The systemic theory is essentially a means whereby an organization shaped on traditional lines can respond to its changing situation in a way that preserves its coherent nature. A diocese (A3, p. 73) that was shaped in peace-time on familial lines was able to respond to the sudden and demanding exigencies of war in a manner that did not destroy the fundamental nature of the body. Likewise, the Church of England, faced with the prospect of adapting to the modern world, might more readily respond on systemic lines, not only because of the theological foundations of the theory but because it would not involve the shattering effects of a charismatic approach or the rationalizing steps implicit in the classical theory.

Charismatic to systemic

The adoption of the systemic approach as a sequel to the charismatic would mean the retaining of the inspiration essential in the latter, but with a fuller conception of the purpose of the church. The response from members would be more intelligent, and conscious rather than being intuitive. The environment would be known through careful inquiry and study, in the light of which the adaptation could be more deliberate. The shape of parish life that emerged in the parish in the new housing area where the mission was held might also have been attained by a study of the sociological situation and the interpretation of this to the members of the church.

Classical to systemic

In the transition from the classical to the systemic, the emphasis is on the continuing structure, which is reshaped in such a way as to allow great flexibility to meet changes in the environment. This was the burden of the consultants' reports on the diocese of Rupert's Land in Canada (Z1, p. 102) and on the National Council of Churches in New York (Booz, Allen, and Hamilton, 1963); it was also the theme of the organizational inquiry in the Anglican Church of Canada and of the Ridley report concerning the Church of England (1956).

Human relations to systemic

Systemic leadership allows for the same kind of intelligent participation that is common in an organization run on the lines of the human relations theory, but adds a clearer perspective on the purpose of the church and on the world in which it lives – such a perspective seemed to be missing in the parish of Gopherwood (Y3, p. 97).

Regression from the systemic

The systemic conception of leadership can be expressed, then, in terms of the continuity that it has with the alternatives it might replace. There are differences that could be stressed: a supporter of the traditional theory may not like change in any form; the classical thinker may want rigidity at all times. However, investigations have shown that the difficulties in attaining the systemic position generally derive not from the desire to cling to a particular feature of an alternative approach, but from the desire to cling to such approaches in their entirety because of the security that people feel when operating in an accustomed way. The first four theories are reasonably well known; the systemic is generally unfamiliar. Hence people adhere to the patterns of operation that they know, and are loath to put their trust in something strange, particularly when their first impression of the alien approach is that it involves the overthrowing of all accepted organizational procedures.

The reorganization in the Anglican Church of Canada was to some extent thwarted by the persistence of the structure of departments in the central offices. In the diocese of Rupert's Land (Z1, p. 102), the accepted committee procedures (criticized in the report) were preferred by the synod to the new way of operating through project groups and expert officers. In a later phase of the diocese of Ripon (Z2, p. 104), there was a resurgence of the basic traditional character of church life and of the episcopal office. The vicar who was involved in fund-raising for the church school had the opportunity at a later stage of adopting a more coherent approach through relating this activity to the total management of the school; but instead he continued on his charismatic way by arousing enthusiasm on the occasion of the centenary of the school and the visit of the archbishop. In all these cases, irrespective of the theory involved, there were signs of a regression from a possible systemic position to what were known methods of operation.

The first step in adopting the systemic approach must be teaching about the theory itself so that is is seen as a *modus operandi* that has an integrity of its own and has foundations in both management thinking and theology. Failure to convey these cardinal points will mean that any attempt to put the theory into practice will be met by efforts to revert to better-known methods of operation whose acceptability rests not on organizational or doctrinal inquiry but on mere familiarity.

COEXISTENT ORGANIZATIONAL PATTERNS

The preceding section examined the problems involved in the transition from one pattern of organizational life to another; and a notable feature was the difficulty caused by the persistence of one mode of operation in the régime of a new leader whose administrative behaviour was different. This situation can become endemic when the patterns are not merely in sequence but coexistent; and such coexistence can be at the same or at diverse levels of organization.

POWER STRUCTURES AT THE SAME LEVEL

The problem

At any one level of organizational life, it is possible for two or more power structures or governing authorities to exist. They can each claim full authority over all areas of the organization's activities; they can be based on different forms of legitimation; they can be administered under differing patterns of leadership; and they can have the power to thwart each other.

The question of dual power structures is not a peculiarly ecclesiastical issue. The decisions of a parliament may be the decisions of the majority party acting independently; likewise, the policy of a political party, though overtly determined on a democratic basis, can spring from the pressures of a caucus or of an influential group behind the scenes. Organizations as diverse as potato-marketing associations and hospital boards have been dominated by sectarian interests which have infiltrated the governing bodies. The administration of the city of Ottawa is complicated by the presence of rival federal, provincial, and municipal authorities.

Nevertheless, the coexistence of power structures is of very great importance in churches because of the emphasis on the doctrine of the unity of the church: there can be no real unity if at the very centre of its life there are forces pulling in opposing directions. Besides, one or other of the rival governing authorities is normally rooted in the theology of the ministry.

Illustrations

The phenomenon of coexistent power structures is universal in the church. It is manifest in America and England and in many other countries; it occurs in most ecclesiastical bodies; it is common to the several church polities – episcopal, presbyterian, congregational; and illustrations can be found at all levels of church organization. The following examples range from the local to the international level.

The issue is clearly seen in parishes of the Church of England where the priesthood has, besides its theological basis, an inherited authority which is backed by legal force in the form of the parson's freehold. Alongside this power structure a second authority has been created since the passing of the Enabling Act in 1919: parochial church councils have been brought into being, with an overt democratic emphasis, and these bodies have rights over an area more or less coterminous with that of the parish priest. There can be harmony when priest and council work together; but the duality makes conflict a very real possibility. A priest can act in a way that is virtually independent of the council's wishes;

and a difficult council can obstruct almost everything that a parish priest tries to do.

In local churches where the congregational or democratic polity is the norm, the problem is partly overcome by virtue of the minister's being essentially the paid servant of the congregation; but difficulties are likely to arise whenever the minister feels that he has certain rights deriving from his ordination to the ministry. There is a partial solution for this dichotomy in the presbyterian form of government where the governing body is constituted by pastor and elders together, and this joint body has a legitimation in the presbyterian doctrine of the ministry; but the pastor still has independent rights in the realm of preaching.

On the diocesan level in England there is the same duality as that which exists on the parochial level. The bishop has an authority based on the doctrine of episcopacy; it is embedded in the tradition of the church and in the law which governs it; and around the bishops have been built up power structures consisting in many cases of archdeacons and rural deans who meet as a body to consider diocesan policy. Alongside this structure is that arising from the Enabling Act consisting of the diocesan conference and its ancillary bodies. There are various possible relationships: a bishop may work in with and follow the general mind of the diocesan conference; however, he may use his right of veto by voting as the only member of the house of bishops against the wishes of the houses of clergy and laity; he also may work quite independently of the new diocesan machinery. In one diocese, all the vital decisions were made by the bishop's hierarchy; the secretary of the Board of Finance was not even privy to the meetings; and the board had the invidious task of trying to cope with many unforeseen demands. In another case, the influence of the secretary of the Board of Finance was so dominant that the bishop himself had to bow to his decisions (X5, p. 88).

Such conflict of interest is possible wherever the traditional English conception of episcopacy has been transplanted. For instance, in the consultants' report on an Anglican diocese in Canada (Z1, p. 102), it was said (p. 4) that 'the superimposition of a multiplicity of advisory, executive and specialized agencies upon a structure having a heritage of hierarchy and absolute authority has not, we understand, met with complete success'. Nevertheless, the problem is not solely within the English heritage. Where the norm is democratic synodical government, there is always the possibility of clash should a church leader attempt to assert independent rights which he considers to be an essential part of his office.

The difficulty is found also on the national level in the Church of England. The joint traditional authority of the bishops and clergy – by virtue of the doctrine of the ministry implied in their orders – is preserved in the Convocations of Canterbury and York; yet alongside this governing structure there has been created the machinery of the Church Assembly, with its three houses of bishops, clergy, and laity. Not only has there been duplication, involving, for instance, dual attendance by many bishops and clergy, but there has been the possibility of conflict. However, the tension has been avoided very largely by the adoption of the theologically questionable division of functions between the spiritual and the material (X1, p. 85).

The same situation is being faced in the Roman Catholic Church on all levels at which consideration is being given to participative rather than authoritarian decision-making, the latter being based on the theological doctrines of the priesthood, the episcopate, and the papacy. At the international level of the papacy the problem is illustrated most publicly. The first Vatican Council defined the authority of the pope in terms of the infallibility decree; the second Vatican Council wrestled with the question of the authority of the bishops. The joint authority of the bishops is expressed through the medium of a council; and such a council is by its very constitution a rival power structure to the papacy itself. The papal structure has always found it difficult to accommodate the conciliar movement; and perhaps the most notable recent example of tension was the refusal of Pope Paul VI to allow the second Vatican Council to vote on a decree when it seemed that the majority of the council might reach a decision that would have been an embarrassment to papal policy.

The solution

One of the solutions to the problem is to accept the coexistence and learn to live with the anomaly. This has been the method adopted in the Church of England.

There the situation has been not merely dual power structures, but a multiplicity of governing authorities. Such a feature is common in an organization that has developed on the lines of the traditional theory: in the diocese of Ripon before the Second World War (A3, p. 73), a large number of semi-autonomous bodies were at work in the diocese; on the national level there are so many points at which power is exercised as to give the appearance of confusion. It is very difficult for people brought up in the American tradition to see how the Church of England can operate at all with this bewildering diffusion of authority; and such people can become very impatient and eager to suggest reforms. The multiple power structure has also been the butt of ridicule in the somewhat satirical book by Paul Ferris (1962). Nevertheless, the situation is comprehensible in terms of the traditional theory: all the parts fit into a coherent whole with each part doing that portion of the total task for which it was originally created; and so many parts operate according to the traditional approach to decision-making that serious conflict in organizational character is minimized.

In this way, it is possible to live with the anomaly of dual or multiple power structures provided there is a general consensus to operate in the light of the common traditional theory; and it might seem that the same arrangement could be made in terms of operating according to any one of the other theories. However, the key point is that there can be no such agreement because, in any one situation, the rival governing authorities are, by heritage or constitution, based on different theories. The traditional is the norm in England; whereas the Life and Liberty Movement was of a charismatic character, and it developed into a governing structure overtly shaped according to the democratic theory but often operated on classical lines. The conciliar movement in the Roman Catholic Church is an expression of the human relations theory and it stands over against the standard classical shape of the papacy. The presbyteral arrangement allows for the independent rights of the preacher, perhaps of a charismatic character, against a background of democratically determined policy. In a congregational setting, a minister may exercise authority in either traditional or classical terms in the face of the general mind of the congregation. Hence the very duality has an inherent possibility of conflict, and the English method is, at its best, only a way of ameliorating the situation, not of solving it.

Besides this difficulty, there is the theological problem of the unity of the church. It is granted that in the traditional approach there can be a unity of all the diverse parts; and such a position is tenable within the limits of the traditional theory. However, it is a non-reflective unity; and once structural issues become a matter of conscious concern, then the former conception can no longer be sustained. And the fact of the matter is that any new form of structure necessarily springs from deliberate action on the conscious level, with the result that the new organization exists outside the kind of unity envisaged in the traditional theory.

In passing, it is interesting to note how the growing awareness in England about matters of ecclesiastical administration has been accompanied by organizational developments bearing on multiple power structures. Two important missionary societies have merged into one; and the dichotomy between the Church Assembly and the convocations was being closed in the 1960s by the temporary expedient of inviting the opinion of the house of laity in the Church Assembly with regard to the Anglican-Methodist conversations which were before the convocations, and by long-term plans for the development of synodical government, which is common in America and in other parts of the world.

Nevertheless, there has been the fear that a solution in terms of unifying the duality would lead to a situation on classical lines – and this has always been a real danger in the American scene. Yet unity need not necessarily be for the sake of centralization and uniformity. The systemic alternative is unity for the sake of expressing the essential character of the church and its total commitment to its mission in the world. The unified structure would thus express in organizational terms the basic theology of the church; but the necessity to operate in terms of the systemic rather than the classical theory would remain.

This manner of operating would allow for a deeper resolution of the problem of duality. The essential point is that the leadership of clergy at all levels has a legitimation in the doctrine of the ministry; and by independent exercise of this authority they can act in a way contrary to any other created power structure. The systemic solution is to see that the function of the leader need not be to exercise an authority in rivalry with (or in opposition to) the remainder of the organization, but rather to make a contribution that is necessary and beneficial to the whole body. His role is to fulfil the monitoring function. In this way he is able to exercise a full and satisfying ministry, and his work is related to the functions of ministering and maintaining. Even though these two functions (and especially the last) may be subject to the alternative lay or elected form of government, the leader can obviate any clash of interest by concentrating his attention on those external factors to which both he and the whole organization must respond. On these lines, a parish priest towards his council or a minister towards his congregational body can perform the monitoring function; likewise, a bishop in a diocese, or an archbishop on the national level, has the task of clarifying the church's purpose, and of interpreting the character of the external world in relation to the whole diocesan or national life (e.g. Z2, p. 104). An instance of this on the international level was the papacy of Pope John XXIII whose concern was with the church's fulfilling its role in the modern world rather than with the promulgation of infallible decrees.

POWER STRUCTURES AT DIFFERENT LEVELS

Illustrations of the problem

Another problem is to be found where power structures, instead of coexisting at the same level of organization, exist at two or more different levels. This situation is endemic to churches in that the structures at some levels have a theological legitimation, whereas the structures at other levels have no such foundation. The development of organization at these latter levels is considerably hampered by the lack of a theological basis.

One of the most comprehensive illustrations of levels of church organization is that given by Spencer (1963) of the Roman Catholic Church. He pointed out the existence of three levels: parochial, diocesan, and papal; and went on to show the need for intermediate structures at deanery, national, and regional or continental levels. He was concerned with such classical concepts as 'the span of control' and 'the chain of command' in the organizational pyramid. He also showed (1966) that in the Middle Ages the several structures corresponded to sociocultural realities: the parish corresponded to the village, the deanery to the district, the diocese to the town with its hinterland, the province to the mediaeval nation. However, the difficulty about establishing intermediate structures is that they do not have the theological basis that the others have: the parish is related to the doctrine of the priesthood, the diocese to episcopacy, the world-wide structure to the papacy. Moreover, the development of a deanery could involve the weakening of the authority of the diocesan bishop and the overriding of the authority of the parish priest; likewise, the creation of a national or regional structure could detract from papal status and usurp rights of diocesan bishops. Thus the organizing of such intermediate structures would be faced with a serious handicap.

Other churches, such as the Presbyterian, which have developed a world-wide organization have done so on the basis of an association of member bodies or of a constitutional relationship rather than on a foundation of doctrine. Likewise, the Anglican Communion has taken cognizance of national groupings and has created an international structure on the basis of common consent and mutual heritage: there is a governing body consisting of the primates of the national churches; and some attempt has been made to provide for growth on regional lines in the programme of Mutual Responsibility and Interdependence.

However, it is primarily on the national level that Anglican churches face the kind of problem envisaged in this section. Development on this level involves some form of nation-wide organization together with the appointment of a national leader generally called a 'primate'; but the diocese is the level of organization that is theologically legitimated – in the doctrine of episcopacy; and so the problem is about the status of the national organization and leader. It is solved in England by the historic position of the sees of Canterbury and York; and so on traditional rather than on legal grounds the respective archbishops have a great degree of authority. Any thought about further provincial measures in England has almost always been in terms of elevating other ancient sees to archiepiscopal rank. However, in newer countries such as Canada and Australia there is not so much historical precedent, although primacy has been advocated in the case of Sydney, the first diocesan seat in Australia. Diocesan, rather than national, organization has come first, and each diocese has become an independent jurisdiction. Hence any primatial expansion tends to encroach upon the exercise of *episcope* by bishops in their territorial areas; and so the primatial office is somewhat nominal – the influence of the primate depends on the calibre of the man in office and on the support he is given. The primate is also inhibited in his office by having territorial responsibilities: in a report in Canada it was insisted that the bishop should have some geographical area in or around Toronto; and in Australia the General Synod approved the extension of the list of diocesan bishops eligible for election to the primacy but would not countenance a non-diocesan bishop on the lines of the presiding bishop of the Protestant Episcopal Church in the United States. The latter has no diocesan responsibilities: his function is virtually that of chief executive on the national level.

Another church in which the same basic problem is seen is the United Church of Canada. There is a theological legitimation of its local organization in the congregational polity which it inherited from one of its constituent parts; at the presbyteral level, there is a foundation in the doctrine contributed by the presbyterian element; but it also has developed organization on the conference and on the national levels. There was an interesting situation in the 1960s in the British Columbia Conference which consisted of a number of presbyteries. The conference began to assume more and more importance in the life of the church since it could supervise work on a much wider scale than the presbytery; and eventually an executive officer was appointed for the conference. A satisfactory working arrangement seemed to evolve between this officer and those at the presbyteral level; it depended on goodwill but it could easily have been vitiated by high-handed action by the executive or by the jealous guarding of rights by presbyteral leaders.

A classic study of the same situation in a congregational setting was given by Harrison (1959) when he investigated the American Baptist Convention. The theology of the Baptist Church was such that all authority was vested in the separate congregations; any development beyond the congregation had no legitimate foundation in theology. Yet the congregations together had to establish an organization on the national level for the sake of extending their work on a greater scale; a structure on the lines of the classical theory was created, and great power was exercised by the officials of the central office. Harrison felt that one way to curb the excessive bureaucratic control was for the member churches to recognize the central office and to give it a constitutional basis so that there were some restraints imposed on the officers.

How to make rural deaneries effective has been a perennial issue in the Church of England. The basic weakness of organization at this level is that the deanery is intermediate between the parish and the diocese and lacks the theological and legal foundations that these levels possess. Some legal powers have been given to rural deans; but the office itself is not attached to any doctrine of the ministry. Sometimes rural deans are associated with the ancient episcopal authority and derive some prestige therefrom; at other times they fit into a hierarchy conceived on classical lines and exercise authority delegated from the bishop.

Within a parish there can be problems of organization based on questions of theological or legal legitimacy; an instance is given in the following extract from a parish management study (Rudge, 1966b, p. 18):

> The fact that the major parish of Seacroft was created before the separate areas became parishes means that there is a constitution provided for the governing of the major parish in the provisions of the Representation of the Laity Measure, 1956, for Parochial Church Councils; but there is no provision for the government of churches (or areas of ministry) within a parish.
>
> Had the major parish been created after the several areas had become parishes, then there would have been a form of government for the several churches, each having a PCC; but there would be no constitution for the major parish as such.
>
> The fact that the development in Seacroft has been in the former pattern has some important governmental consequences. The only legal governing body is the PCC, and its chairman – the vicar – is the only clergyman in the parish with legal authority; by contrast, the existing church committees are unofficial, and their normal chairmen – the priests-in-charge – have no legal standing. Thus there is likely to be a strong tendency for the real power in the parish to be in the hands of the vicar and PCC to the detriment of the church committees and their clergy. (Had the development been according to the second pattern, all the power would have been vested in the local bodies and the local clergymen; and the central governing body and the person in charge of the whole parish would have been at a disadvantage.)

The organizational problem presented here also had ramifications in the realm of personnel policy (p. 25):

> The fact that the development of the parish has taken its present course, instead of the creation of a major parish out of several existing parishes, has had implications in the realm of stipends. Had the latter course been pursued, those clergy attached to churches would now have incumbent stipends; as it is, they only have curates' stipends although they have been recognized as having special responsibility and so since July 1st have been paid at the special rate for holding such responsibility – £900 p.a. as against £1,050 p.a. for an incubent. Thus the present staff are victimized by the chance circumstances of the way in which the parish has developed. If the major parish were composed of small village parishes, the members of staff would automatically have incumbent stipends; but with much greater responsibilities than clergy in many small parishes have, the staff are not granted incumbent stipends.

The question of the status of a whole ecclesiastical area as against the status of constituent parts is faced over and over again in the development of group and team ministries; and it has been the occasion of comment in a study of the ministry in the Stevenage area (Price, 1963).

The theme in all these examples is the same: some levels of church organization are anchored in theology; others, which are not, are generally at a disadvantage. The basis of the issue is the doctrine of the ministry; but the solution is not just learning to live with an intractable problem.

The solution

The answer lies in seeing that there can be a theological legitimation for those levels of government that do not already have it; but this can be realized only when it is recognized that the doctrines of the ministry, which provide the foundation of some levels of organization, are in fact couched in terms of one or other of the organizational theories.

In the Anglican scene, episcopacy is generally expressed in terms of the traditional theory: *episcope* can be real only when confined to a distinct limited geographical area called a diocese; likewise, priesthood is restricted to the boundaries of a parish marked on a map. The geographical element is also present in the Roman conception, though the classical emphasis on authority appropriate to a place in the pyramidal hierarchy is dominant. But it must not be supposed that episcopacy is in its essence limited by such geographical or hierarchical features. Archbishop Coggan of York exercised a notable ministry in sponsoring the Feed the Minds Campaign, and this has taken him beyond the diocese of York, beyond the province of York, and even outside accustomed ecclesiastical fields altogether. In the Celtic church, it was the abbot rather than the bishop who was the ecclesiastical authority and his realm was defined in familial as much as geographical terms. In the Eastern Orthodox Church, it is not unknown for several bishops with overlapping jurisdictions to be living in the same place; and there are parallel Anglican and Roman Catholic episcopates in most countries of the world – evidence that bishops do not have in fact exclusive and complete geographical rights.

Instead of being couched in traditional or classical terms, it is possible for the doctrine of the ministry to be stated in systemic terms. *Episcope* belongs to the whole church and is to be exercised wherever there is a task to be performed; around the task and situation, the organization can be constructed and the episcopal function expressed. The diocesan bishop exercises oversight in relation to the tasks that belong to the area that constitutes his diocese; other responsibilities are related to the wider area of a nation – for instance, Canada or Australia – and on this level the primate can fulfil his *episcope*; and he should be able to do so without having the encumbrance of a particular local territory. The office could be held in this way without the fears associated with the American pattern, provided the primate exercises his leadership in systemic rather than classical terms. The relationship between a national leader and a diocesan bishop would be determined by reference to the task – the task that belongs to the whole church rather than to one man, and that is shared by reference to the situation so as to see where it can be done most effectively. For example, the relation of the church to a national government should be the responsibility of the primate or the presiding bishop rather than of the local bishop in whose territory the seat of government happened to be. The primate would exercise a theological role of the oversight of the body of Christ on the national level with respect to the appropriate tasks; likewise, the basis of the diocesan bishop's office would be the monitoring of the church at the diocesan level with regard to the responsibilities to be fulfilled in that area. In this way, the national office would not be at a disadvantage compared with the diocesan position – as is the case when the latter is expressed in terms of the traditional or the classical theory.

The problem of the malfunctioning of rural deaneries may also be solved by reference to task and situation. Most deaneries are moribund because there is no real work for them to do: they can be regarded simply as places where clergy can meet together. However, in terms of the systemic theory, the deanery would be related to an area where there is a very real task to be done, and so there would be some substance to the deanery organization. In the diocese of Southwark, an attempt was made to reshape the diocesan structure to fit the administration of the new Greater London Council; and so some deaneries were made coterminous with the boroughs with a view to working in such fields as education, which were borough responsibilities. There was also a need to adapt to smaller areas within the boroughs which were communities of interest, and so the sub-deaneries were reshaped to meet this need. The main difficulty was in imposing a structure shaped partly in classical and partly in democratic terms on a situation that required structures of a systemic character. When deaneries are thus related to significant areas where there is a field of responsibility, there is the possibility of new life; and in this arrangement the rural dean would become the person who exercised the monitoring function with respect to items of concern appropriate to his area. The office of rural dean would then have a theological basis in the doctrine of the ministry and in the doctrine of church and society; and the organizational structure would have the same legitimation as have the parish and the diocese.

Spencer (1966) noted that the intermediate levels of organization in the Roman Catholic Church which he desired to develop had geographical counterparts in the Middle Ages; and they could have a similar relevance in the modern world. Within the terms of the classical theory, it would be difficult to establish effective organization at these stages because of the implied threat to the authority of higher or lower levels which have a foundation in the classical doctrine of the ministry; however, a development on systemic lines might not be an impossibility. Some of the informal moves on the national level, as in the hierarchy in the United States, are in this direction; and Gallicanism has had a long history in the church in France. It is recognized that there are issues to be faced which are essentially national in character, and on this basis a theologically viable structure might be created.

The conclusion is that problems deriving from coexistent power structures at different levels of organization, though intractable when seen in terms of the traditional or classical theories, may be capable of resolution through the application of the systemic theory of ecclesiastical administration.

CHURCH UNION

The problems relating to coexistent organizational structures that have been hitherto considered are of long standing in the church; but there is another relevant area of concern in which the interest is more recent, namely, that of church union.

Only limited attention has been paid to the organizational aspects of this issue. A notable work on the subject is *Institutionalism and Church Unity* (Ehrenstrom and Muelder, 1963), together with a Faith and Order document (1963) based on the case-studies in the book. This document in itself is a valuable contribution to the study of ecclesiastical administration (see also Dady, 1961).

The topic of church union is becoming increasingly important. The Anglican-Methodist conversations are going forward in England; the creation of the Uniting Church is a serious possibility in Australia and there is also the question of Anglican participation; and negotiations between the Anglican Church of Canada and the United Church of Canada have been reopened. All schemes of union such as these involve major organizational and administrative issues somewhat on the lines under discussion in this chapter. A union means the coexistence of two or more organizational structures alongside each other; such structures are likely to be different from one another because of their different origins and polities, although an interesting line of sociological inquiry has shown that, irrespective of source or doctrine, many churches have in fact assumed a common organizational character. The fact that this is so has to a large extent prepared the way for the possibility of union; and the prominence of organizational issues means that union can be studied in terms of organizational theory.

Union, according to the traditional theory, would involve the bringing together of several different traditions into the one church; but such traditions might be continued almost as though they were separate. In the Church of South India, four main Christian traditions were united: Anglican, Presbyterian, Methodist, Congregational; but it was noted in a subsequent review of the situation that many of the local churches had merely continued in their former ways without any real committal to a complete union or at least to a sharing of traditions (Rajaiah D. Paul, 1958, p. 213).

To a certain extent, schemes of union have been the product of some exceptionally gifted men who have wielded great influence not only in their own churches but in the others as well: Bishop Azariah of Dornakal in the negotiations for union in South India is an instance. The importance of such men can be gauged by noting how, when they die or go elsewhere, negotiations can slow down or slump completely. Both the North Indian and the South Indian schemes yield evidence of this.

A union on classical lines would involve a formal, legal relationship between the participating bodies, leading to a standardization of church life on the lines of another act of uniformity; but perhaps the history subsequent to the original Act of Uniformity is a sufficient warning against this kind of approach to church unity. Nevertheless, fear of domination, even if not of uniformity, has been a real factor in the Anglican-Methodist conversations in England; to some people the scheme has appeared as a 'take-over' bid by the Church of England, which might not allow the distinctive Methodist contributions to have their rightful place in the new body.

An approach to unity in the light of the human relations theory would mean the seeking of a compromise which would keep all the participants happy, perhaps in terms of the lowest common denominator. This, together with government pressure, seemed to be the basis of the war-time scheme of union in Japan and was the ground on which the Nippon Sei Ko Kai refused to join.

Part of the systemic approach would be to shape the several structures on the lines of the systemic theory so that their union would be made easier; but the union would have to be more than a mechanistic joining of systemic-type organizations. The real union would be the growing together in the common commitment to the church's purpose in the situation in which the church lived. The common character of the purpose in the identical situation would mean that the common life would develop out of the response to these contextual factors. The process would be facilitated by recognition of the theological basis to this approach and by the way in which the systemic theory throws new light on such doctrines as that of the ministry which have so often been stumbling blocks in the path to union.

CHAPTER 7

Ordinary Administrative Issues

The chapters on the general shape of church life and the discussion of the various problems of policy or polity have served to show something of the wide connotation of the term 'administration' which was advocated at the outset; but no administrative study is complete without reference to the issues which are ordinarily described as 'administrative': finance, buildings, personnel. These items belong to the maintaining function of a system; and one outcome of the study is to see that this function has its rightful dignity even though it is supportive of the main activity of the organization. Because of this worthiness, these topics merit full treatment; and this can be given in the light of the fundamental theory that underlies ecclesiastical administration. The issues cannot be considered in isolation, as mere appendages to organizational studies and as though they had a rationale of their own; the unity of this study is in the fact that the very character of financial management, building policy, and personnel management is derived from the theory which is relevant to the whole organizational life. Five theories have been considered, and for each there is a corresponding approach to the several ordinary administrative topics.

FINANCIAL MANAGEMENT

The traditional policy

The traditional policy is based on the unreflecting continuance of what has been done before. The annual accounts are a record of the financial transactions of the preceding year, and the assumption is that the future year's activities will follow the same course. The statement of the past is virtually the budget for the new year; there is probably no formally drafted budget at all. Financial control is not so much by formal regulation or fiscal watchfulness as by the implicit understanding that those who disburse the money will continue as they have done in the past. Thus the decisions are not made by a central monetary authority but by those semi-autonomous bodies that make up the total organization. The accounts are really the summation of a multitude of virtually separate activities between which there is no formal relationship – they just cohere within the tradition or the family life of the organization; and each activity has its own income and expenditure. The balance between the two arises from the long period of stability in the organization. Any new needs that may arise are met from sources outside the normal income: by tapping an endowment or a special fund, by private benefaction, by appeals associated with important events such as anniversaries or centenaries, by running special money-raising functions.

The foregoing statement is illustrated in the case of the diocese of Ripon (A3, p. 73) and in the following review of an actual parish situation (Rudge, 1966a, pp. 430–2):

> In the parish of Nettlewood, there was no indication in the minutes of the Parochial Church Council that the parish finances were operated on a conscious budgetary principle at this time [1956]. The main financial document was the churchwardens' account, which was the statement of receipts and expenditure for the twelve months ending on December 31. The stability of the main items on both sides over a period of years indicated that, although a formal budget had not been presented, there was an understanding that the finances of the ensuing year would closely follow those of the previous period.
>
> There was little significant direction by the vicar or the council in the actual shaping of the financial state of the parish. The accounts represented the summation of many independent purposes and activities. The income was grouped under three main headings. The first was the Free-Will Scheme with its dual objects of general expenses and the church overseas, and in 1956 the income amounted to £1,500. The other items were Collections for General Expenses (£581) and Special Collections (£245); these embraced a multitude of sources of income.
>
> The expenditure was grouped under four headings:
>
> The Church in the Parish
> The Church at Home
> The Church Overseas
> General Charities.
>
> The first contained the normal parish expenses, and there was a consistency in the figures through the years; the amount in 1956 was £2,000.

In the second group were eight different channels of outlay: some, such as the diocesan quota, were of obligation; others were of a more voluntary nature depending on how much happened to be collected for a particular cause. The total was £338.

The latter characteristic was particularly true of the items grouped under the heading of The Church Overseas. Eleven different missionary funds were supported to the total extent of £353; and, although the general emphasis was fairly consistent, the amounts and the directions in which they were given indicated little attempt to formulate a policy of missionary giving. Further indication of this was in the fact that another table of missionary giving was printed showing the total giving from the whole parish, and it included a further £140 from sources outside the range of the council.

The contributions to General Charities showed the same randomness; the figure here was £57.

In addition, there was a separate account called the Fabric Fund which had an income from dividends and interest amounting to £121 and an outlay of £458 on repairs and renewals. There was also a distinct Sunday school account showing collections of £107 and expenses of £94. The former of these funds was under the control of the council but the latter was not. However, the Sunday school was dependent at times on contributions from the churchwardens' account, and there was a rule that any surplus in excess of £10 in the Sunday school account should be transferred to the churchwardens' account. A move to revoke this rule was defeated at the council meeting on April 4, 1957.

In 1956 the proportion of the total expenditure spent on the local church was approximately three-quarters, and about one-eighth was given, respectively, to the church in the diocese and the church abroad. This was not a matter of policy: it was an *ex post facto* statement.

The charismatic theory

The financial policy associated with the charismatic theory is related to the magnetic personality of the leader and the particular content of his intuitions. The special objectives such a leader supports figure prominently in the accounts to the point of requiring a disproportionate amount of the organization's resources to pay for them. The normal source of income is through appeals related to the specific objectives, with the hope that the personal qualities of the leader and the worthiness of the causes will attract the support of the public irrespective of whether the people are in any formal relationship with the organization. The result of the appeal depends on the compliance or otherwise of these people: a successful appeal is likely to be drawn from a wide range of contributors; but should the charisma wane, then the burden falls all the more heavily on the few who are still interested.

Typical of this method was the policy of a bishop who first of all espoused the cause of children's homes in his diocese; he used every opportunity to spread the idea and in due course attracted wide support for the project. The homes and hostels were eventually built; and their subsequent cost became a normal and accepted charge on the diocesan budget, although some people who were still enthusiastic about the idea made direct contributions to the homes (particularly because such gifts were tax free). Having achieved his first objective, the bishop was carried away with the idea of establishing a post-graduate theological library in the national capital for the benefit of the whole church. Now this became his absorbing interest; and every occasional address and sermon eventually touched on the subject. Appeals were made; subscriptions were sought on many sides; a private benefactor fired with the same vision gave substantially; and diocesan resources were diverted into this single project with the result that, in his final year in the see, the diocese was a very considerable sum in debt.

A similar approach was followed by the vicar who opted for a government-aided school in his parish. After finding some interest in surrounding parishes, he prompted the calling of a public meeting at which an appeal was launched. The attractive force of his personality and the magnetic quality of the project were the factors that influenced people to give their support, at least in the initial period; but the postponement of the building plans soon cut off this source of income. Some time later, when hopes of building were renewed, the policy was again to appeal publicly and widely for funds, though there was little response at this stage; even when the committee had become defunct and the scheme was renewed on a new footing, the vicar still relied on people's spontaneous enthusiasm which he tried to stir up in connection with the centenary of the school and the visit of the archbishop.

The classical method

The essence of a classical kind of financial policy is the centralized control of both income and expenditure. All resources and demands are channelled through a single budgetary operation (X4, p. 87). On the one hand, income is derived from quotas levied on constituent bodies according to a scale of apportionment; and on the expenditure side disbursements are made to claimant bodies according to a formula devised by the financial authority. This authority is the dominant governing body in the organization; that is, the maintenance function directs rather than supports the activities of the organization; and in this authoritative body it is the officials who are the most influential people.

An instance of the predominance of the financial authority is seen in the Church of England on the diocesan level. The body entrusted with the continuing government of the church is the Board of Finance; and its position as a legally constituted body can give it much more than a supportive role – in one case, the secretary of the board virtually directed the policy of the diocese irrespective of the wishes of the bishop (X5, p. 88).

The methods of professional fund-raising – common in America, generally accepted in Australia, and becoming more widespread in England – are often couched in terms of the classical theory: the campaigns involve a major rationalization of the resources of a parish; a massive organization is created; the target is expressed in terms of the money needed for a series of projects; card indexes, files, and record sheets fill the parish office; and although direction as to what people should give is eschewed, there are often misgivings about the kind of approach that is made. After the initial canvass, there is a follow-up of those whose support lapses; and every three years or so, there is a further campaign. Fund-raising thus becomes a series of major discrete steps, for each of which the organizational machinery is specially set in motion.

The human relations approach

The human relations approach is to some extent a reaction against the impersonal methods of the classical theory. The voluntary element is stressed: giving depends on free will rather than direction; people should give 'what they feel like giving'. Sometimes this may mean the rejection of any scheme involving deliberate and conscientious support; but where such methods are accepted, the freedom of choice is emphasized.

This point of view need not mean the abandonment of the unified budget of the classical theory; but the human element would be introduced. Instead of the budget consisting of mere strings of figures, the items would be presented and explained in such a way as to show the human and personal side of the causes being supported. The inclusion of overseas missionary work, for example, in the one budget can give the impression of neglecting the intimate connections that are forged between the giving and receiving churches – a feature that missionary societies in England have always tried to stress – and it is often argued in England that the entering of these items, according to the common American pattern, in what appears to be an impersonal list of figures is to destroy something that is precious in the life of the church. Hence, there needs to be a considerable public relations programme as part of the activity of financial management to overcome the somewhat soulless character of the classical method.

Another feature of the classical approach that would be rejected from a human relations standpoint is the dominance of officials in the determination of financial policy; this should be more in the hands of elected representatives who have the right to say how their money and that of their constituents should be used.

The systemic way

All the major characteristics of a system form the basis of the systemic way of financial management; and on each point there is a noteworthy contrast with the practices appropriate to the classical or traditional approaches.

A system is essentially a unity, and so, in financial terms, there is a unified form of management. The basis is an 'all-in-one' budget, not for the sake of centralized control and efficiency of operation, but for the sake of expressing the unity of the church; there is a single, unified process comprehending all income and expenditure. On the income side, it represents the commitment by members – be they individuals in a local church, or parishes in a diocese, or dioceses in a national church – who, through regular offerings, pledge themselves to the work of the whole body. On the expenditure side, all items are included because there is but one unifying purpose to which the organization is committed; the distribution is made according to the various responsibilities that the whole body has, not as single items for support, but as expressions of a common purpose. For instance, the inclusion of 'missions' in a single budget, as is common in America and Australia, is a recognition of the whole church's dedication to 'mission' in all its forms; to leave overseas responsibilities to those who happen to be interested or who care to drop a small coin in a mission box is to deny the world-wide involvement of all Christians. In a particular diocese, the ministry of social responsibility was eventually brought within the diocesan budget – instead of being financed as formerly by a special appeal – with a view to demonstrating that this area of work was a rightful part of the church's total mission; the department would henceforth have, not only direct financial support from the diocese, but also the strength of the whole diocese's commitment to its work.

Within the wholeness of a system, financial management is a part; but it is not the private endeavour of the maintaining function, apart from the remainder of the organization. So often fund-raising campaigns are purely isolated money-making drives separate from the life and activity of the whole church; and in this way tend to take on classical features. Stewardship, rightly understood, is a way of presenting the challenge of the gospel; and a stewardship committee is as much within the ministering function as the maintaining function. There is an interdependence between these two functions as there is also between income and expenditure. The latter point can be seen in this way: the level of income is dependent on the level of giving by parishioners; this in turn is linked with the strength of their convictions; this is related to how well the challenge of discipleship is put before people; such evangelism necessitates the outlay of funds to support the work – but from this expenditure, new sources of income may arise. The interplay between the two functions is an important part of systemic financial management. So, too, is the responsiveness of the financial authority to the new horizons of the organization's work which are interpreted through the monitoring function; instantaneous response is needed for the financing of new ventures, and the method of management must be sufficiently flexible to cope with this kind of situation. The all-in-one budget enables a response of the whole organization to be made to such needs; and a continuous procedure, rather than a somewhat inflexible annual arrangement, can facilitate this. The yearly items of income and expenditure can be translated into weekly terms; and an up-to-date weekly figure can be a guide to policy on a much shorter term than the annual figures, while at the same time it can be used as a safeguard against rash schemes.

There can also be continuity in the raising of income rather than a series of discrete steps as in a fund-raising campaign on the lines of the classical theory. In a certain parish where there was a high degree of mobility, a continuous canvass programme was instituted whereby newcomers were brought into the scheme within a few weeks of their arrival; they were visited by a canvasser after initial contacts had been made by the minister and ladies of the parish. The steady stream of new support more than compensated for that which was lost through the departure of subscribers. Such loss is felt immediately; but the classical method of campaigning means that new income is often much delayed. In this case, the programme was geared to the situation rather than to a preconceived plan of separate stages. The latter approach, typical of the classical theory, has been prominent in England and Australia with the advent of professional fund-raising in churches; but in the course of time many churches have thought in terms of inviting pledges for an indefinite period rather than for, say, three years, in the hope that the practice of regular giving might become part of a normal Christian life, with the responsibility on the donor of making adjustments in his pledge as his financial position changes. In America, where this practice has been accepted over a longer period, the continuity of contributions and the increase in standards of giving are often effected through the holding of 'Stewardship Sundays' once a year – not as a major new campaign, but as the expression of a continuing and increasing commitment to the work of the church.

The continuance of support is ultimately related to the response of members, freely given, to the total purpose of the church; and it is the responsibility of church leaders continually to interpret this purpose in the light of the changing world situation so that the members are acquainted with the full context within which they express their Christian discipleship.

Some of the points in the systemic way of financial management were evident in the subsequent history of the parish whose traditional orientation was noted earlier. It proved to be no longer possible to maintain the non-reflective type of policy in the face of demands made upon the parish in terms of urgent repairs of considerable magnitude to the church, an increased involvement in the parish school, and the call for support for new churches in the vast housing areas around the city. In spite of some diffidence by members of the church council, it was realized that the only solution was to hold an every-member canvass in the parish. All the organization for a full-scale campaign was created; the canvassing was duly completed; and the level of giving was raised substantially. A purely classical approach, however, was obviated by the way in which the vicar stressed the historic continuity of the parish life and nurtured it in many areas, so that the forward move on the financial front was but part of the growing strength of the Christian community; he also interpreted the new budgeting process as the means by which all the parishioners would be involved in the total mission of the church, whether the work was being done in the parish, in the diocese, or overseas. Beyond the initial campaign, there was a continuing programme of follow-up and the canvassing of newcomers to the parish. Within a very few years, the major needs that had prompted the holding of the canvass had been financed; and, at this stage, the vicar emphasized even more the nature of the church's mission in the world so that the apparent commitment to quantitative and pressing financial ends was transformed into a dedication to the full responsibility of the church in the accomplishment of its purpose. The outcome was that the income was more than maintained, and the parish was able to devote a greater proportion of its resources to work beyond the parish. This policy was now by deliberate choice; and it involved the full commitment of all the members to these wider objectives.

BUILDING POLICY

It is commonly assumed that the main administrative problem about church buildings is their cleaning and maintenance: thus Forder (1947) in his handbook included chapters on the care of the church and the management of parish buildings. Such items are important and should not be neglected; but to concentrate on them is to overlook the fundamental administrative problem of having the right kind of building policy. As in all other areas of administration, there is a distinct building policy appropriate to each of the possible theories of ecclesiastical administration.

The general administrative problem has been noted of how the expression of one or other theory can be perpetuated in a pastoral or financial or personnel policy or in the expectations and hopes of the laity; this issue is all the more acute in the case of buildings because they can represent in an even more permanent way the continuance of a particular theory of management. Moreover, buildings can represent resources that are irretrievably sunk in a particular fixed form.

The traditional policy

This is especially so in the case of the building policy appropriate to the traditional theory. The church building is the physical expression of and witness to the unchangeable nature of the eternal God; and so the building material is brick or preferably stone – materials that have an enduring quality about them. England is dotted with buildings of such character. The distinction between a temporary and a permanent building is noted in ritual terms, too, in that only a permanent structure of enduring materials can be consecrated to the glory of God; timber buildings, by contrast, may only be dedicated.

One of the administrative consequences of this kind of building policy is the financial burden of upkeep thrust upon later generations – hence the extensive 'begging' campaigns in many English cathedrals and churches. There is also strong pressure to have many ancient English churches declared as buildings of historic interest under the care of a national authority. It is argued that the church of the present day should not be burdened with responsibility for buildings that are no longer related to the mission and purpose of the church. One traditional-style church, an anomaly in a huge modern programme of urban redevelopment, has been described as 'not only irrelevant but irreverent'. What were once intended as witnesses to the majesty of the eternal God can become monuments to the irrelevance of His church. An extreme instance of this is in the case of several English villages which were struck by the great plague; as a consequence, the people of the village moved to a more healthy spot a mile or so away and established themselves again. But the churches were of such structure that they could not be removed; and so they have remained on their original sites unto this day, quite separate from the life of the villages of which they were once an integral part. There are, however, exceptions to the immobility of stone buildings – before the waters of Lake Eucumbene in the Snowy Mountains of Australia rose to cover the site of the town of Adaminaby, the whole town including a stone church was moved to a new site and re-erected.

The charismatic policy

The contrast between the charismatic and traditional theories extends to the building policy also. Instead of permanent structures, the emphasis is on temporary premises. Many wandering evangelists erect a tent for the duration of their campaign; or they may hire a public hall or arena. Dr Billy Graham's London campaigns were at Harringay Arena and Earl's Court. Soap-box orators in London's Hyde Park or Sydney's Domain need only their soap box or a portable pulpit.

The classical line

The classical building policy is based on the assumption that the church can shape its own life for its own ends independently of the world and community in which it exists. The extensive school building programme of the Roman Catholic Church in America or England or Australia can be of this type where it leads to an isolation from the rest of the community. The plant built by churches in the United States may appear to be another expression of this policy: compared with the traditional English pattern of a church and an adjacent hall, the typical arrangement in America is the erection of a whole complex of buildings comprising not only the church and its vestries, but halls, choir rooms, classrooms, studies, interview rooms, libraries, lounges, rest rooms, canteens. The idea is to provide every facility that might possibly be required to house the life of a body of people who have a permanent existence in their own right and for their own particular purposes. Something approaching this outlook, though not the scale of building, appears to be fairly common in Canada and Australia, where each church seeks to establish its own private empire.

The human relations approach

Supporters of the human relations approach are less wedded to permanent buildings. Some feel that churches are not needed at all; instead, the informality of a private home is more appropriate to the experiencing of close fellowship – the 'house church' movement is often based on this kind of thinking, and for this no special building is required. Thoughts concerning buildings are not so much about permanence or otherwise but about their shape. Many traditional-style buildings have been redesigned inside to allow for the provision of a nave altar and for the westward position of the celebrant, both of which features express more clearly the fellowship between the people around the altar. This was done in Hollywood (C3, p. 82); but the necessary alterations posed a problem in Seacroft (Y2, p. 95). Where a fresh start is made, the new building is likely to be circular or perhaps octagonal, with seating on several sides of the building around the central altar. There is also an emphasis on the character of the ancillary rooms: instead of a large hall, the preference is for smaller rooms suited to intimate groups rather than crowds, and also for rooms where there is privacy for counselling work. The provision of counselling rooms became a necessity in the 'caring nucleus' policy at Seacroft (Y2, p. 95), and *ad hoc* arrangements were made for social functions at one of the churches.

The systemic policy

The building policy appropriate to the systemic theory is in part based on adaptability. One area in which adaptability is required is in the increasingly close relationship between churches in the œcumenical movement. Agreement may be reached not to duplicate building programmes in the same place; arrangements may be made for the joint use of buildings, or separate facilities may be provided under the one roof. Such policies require considerable flexibility in design and also in management.

Another factor that necessitates flexibility in a building programme is the mobility of people. Whole communities sometimes have to be moved and the church must needs follow: the church was removed stone by stone at Adaminaby in the Snowy Mountains of Australia; in another place this was impossible and so a new church had to be built. Short-term mobility is a feature of construction work on major engineering projects: townships are erected for the duration of the particular contract and then are moved to the next job. Clearly, permanent church buildings would be both wasteful and inappropriate; but temporary structures can be devised that are capable of being moved and yet have some beauty and dignity. There is a longer term mobility in large-scale housing projects which may have a life-span of, say, fifty years. Slum-clearance schemes in inner city areas in England have left many permanent churches high and dry because the churches were built with a much longer life-span than the houses around them; and there is a considerable danger that the same mistake may be made again in the newer housing areas. Churches are built on a much more enduring scale than the surrounding dwellings, so that in the next rebuilding programme the churches may again be left isolated.

The most important element, however, in the systemic conception of a building policy is that of adaptability to the needs of the world around so that the buildings are expressive of the church's role in society. This means more than, for instance, building a kindergarten room primarily for church purposes, and then deciding that it can be used during the week for a day nursery. The buildings should be expressive of the church's creative role in society. To some extent this is the reason behind many American church building complexes. In a society where there is still considerable room for voluntary welfare services – more so than in England's welfare state – the churches serve a very real function in this area, and the buildings are designed to provide the facilities for such a ministry (e.g. Z3, p. 107). Where the welfare services are highly developed as in England, the church needs not no independent plant but buildings related closely to the community centres (e.g. Z4, p. 109). In one vast urban redevelopment scheme, the central community buildings were to be erected by the civic authority, and the church would have its rightful place within the centre in the buildings designed for the re-creation of a whole new community life. The church would be relieved of having huge overheads tied up in buildings and would be able to devote its resources to the provision of staff who could exercise the kind of ministry required in this situation. The concern for ministering would not negate the concern for worship; and in many schemes a large central church is envisaged, operated on an œcumenical basis, as the 'major architectural statement of the Christian presence'.

PERSONNEL MANAGEMENT

A glimpse into Weber's theory (1947) gives some idea of the variety of personnel policies there are according to the several perspectives on management. For instance, in outlining the traditional theory, Weber mentioned the recruitment methods, which are characterized by personal loyalty to the chief, favouritism, and nepotism; he also said that the typical way of renumeration is by maintenance in the household, by allowances in kind, by rights of the use of land in return for services, by the appropriation of specific income and fees, and by the granting of benefices.

His exposition of the charismatic approach indicates a very different perspective on personnel issues (pp. 360–1):

> The administrative staff of a charismatic leader does not consist of 'officials'; . . . there is no such thing as 'appointment' or 'dismissal',

> no career, no promotion. There is only a 'call' . . . There is no hierarchy; the leader merely intervenes in general or in individual cases when he considers the members of his staff inadequate to a task with which they have been entrusted. . . . There is no such thing as a salary or benefice. Disciples or followers tend to live primarily in a communistic relationship with their leader on means which have been provided by voluntary gift.

What Weber briefly touched on can be more fully expounded in relation to the many components of a complete personnel policy.

RECRUITMENT AND TRAINING

Consider such topics as recruitment and training. Selection, according to the traditional view, is as Weber indicated; the subsequent training consists of no formal course but rather the grooming of those who are chosen for the privilege of higher office. The juniors are assigned to work alongside senior men, and the experience gained through this association serves to nurture them in the heritage of the organization.

A charismatic leader is likely to give preference to those who share his vision and enthusiasm; these are qualities that cannot be imparted by a formal programme of training, but rather are caught through close personal connection with the leader. There is not likely to be any specific post-ordination training; and even pre-ordination training may be discounted. The background of leaders in religious bodies that are classed as 'sects' is typical of this kind of policy; and the establishment of colleges and seminaries by such bodies for the training of their ministers is perhaps an indication that the religious body has moved along the sect-church continuum towards being a 'church'.

In the classical theory, importance is placed on the role of administrator. For this, a minister needs to be efficient, well drilled in routine, and very businesslike. Such qualities can be imparted through an intensive programme of training in which the emphasis is on competence for specific tasks. Many American institutions for the training of clergy offer courses in parish administration, the subject being somewhat narrowly conceived in terms of business efficiency, organizational procedures, and legal knowledge. It may also be important to provide such courses on a more advanced level beyond ordination on the lines of those provided in business colleges.

In the terms of the human relations theory, there is a premium on people who are keen and interested, those who would respond to and accept responsibility, those who are intelligent but amateur, those who could act in a representative capacity with ability to discuss and debate. Recruitment is by volunteering; and the training programme would be a broad and general education coupled with experience in public affairs. Any tendency towards an exclusive interest in theology as a technical, vocational subject would militate against the broader approach to theology through the humanities which would be necessary for preparing leaders for the democratic version of this theory. The group approach would demand more specific qualifications such as a knowledge of psychology and psychiatry; and it would also be essential that ministers be 'labbed', a colloquial expression for having participated in a group-life laboratory or 'T-group'. These are intensive courses in group dynamics.

According to the systemic theory, recruitment is to the two separate functions – ministering and maintaining. For the former, the enrolling of candidates and their training would continue in much the same way as at present because this function is already well established and recognized. There may be need to develop more specialist ministries, but at the same time to inculcate a sense of commitment to the purpose of the whole church rather than to a specific task or area. It would also be an advantage for people to acquire flexibility so as to be able to work on a short-term basis and to change working relationships with others; further, an ability to take initiative and explore new avenues would be important so that the ministering work might be shaped in a way appropriate to new horizons interpreted through the monitoring function. An awareness of such potential developments in the ministry is reflected in the creation of places of further education such as the Urban Training Center for Christian Mission in Chicago and the Institute for Advanced Pastoral Studies in Bloomfield Hills, Michigan.

In view of the fact that the maintaining function is clearly distinguishable and requires very different talents, such as financial and personnel management, the recruitment to this would be distinct from that to the ministering function. This is in fact what is happening. In America, men are recruited separately for the position of administrator, and the National Association of Church Business Administrators is undertaking the provision of professional courses and standards. In England also, the engagement of those who fulfil the maintaining function (for example, the secretaries of Boards of Finance) is quite separate from the normal recruitment to the ministry; and the usual practice is to draw on men who have had administrative experience elsewhere, notably in the armed forces. It would be desirable that a more serious and overt policy of recruitment be adopted, and also that a course be provided in this area of responsibility that would enable men to work in an interdependent relationship with those in the ministering function and to respond to the theological and situational perspectives given by the leader.

Recruitment for the monitoring function is not likely to be direct, but rather from the ranks of those already engaged in the ministering function, and to a lesser extent from those in the maintaining function. However, the not uncommon English practice of appointing university professors as bishops is perhaps a pointer to another source of recruitment. In the careers of clergymen, the monitoring function assumes importance when they enter upon a new field of responsibility, such as when a curate takes up his first incumbency, when an incumbent is given the charge of a team or group ministry, when a man is nominated as rural dean, or when somebody is raised to the episcopate. The exercise of such new offices involves monitoring rather than new ministering capacities; and, for such people, courses might be provided at the appropriate times. A proposal for a staff college for the Church of England has been made by John Adair (1962); and a development somewhat on these lines has been started at St George's House, Windsor. The courses for œcumenical secretaries at Boston University and the executive training courses of the National Council of Churches in the United States are also indicative of the kind of training that is desirable for the fulfilling of the monitoring function in the church.

METHODS OF APPOINTMENT

Beyond the stage of recruitment and training, the next step is appointment to office. The contrast between the English and American approaches, as well as the insights of the systemic theory, may be seen from the ensuing comments on the issue of *Crown Appointments and the Church*, to quote the title of a report in England in 1964 which stimulated further argument on a perennial problem there.

Some have felt that the report was too conservative in that it provided only for a clearing away of some legal anomalies and for some widening of consultation; they have desired a more radical step. They have rejected the current method, which has affinity with the traditional theory in that there is emphasis on the part played by the senior figures in church and state, in that the deliberations are private, and in that the procedure is of ancient origin. In its place, the method of election has been proposed, a method which is in keeping with the human relations or democratic theory. The debate in England has been about these alternative methods; and no other approaches have been seriously considered. There may be ways of attaining office that could be classed as 'charismatic' – witness the way in which William Temple came to the leadership of the Life and Liberty Movement (C1, p. 79) – but such are too individualistic to be counted as a policy; nor would classical methods such as open examination according to highly specific standards be countenanced for higher offices in the church. However, a contribution may be made in the light of the systemic theory.

The emphasis on the task of the church and on the need for leaders to be fitted to their responsibilities means that the debate about the two methods must be seen in the light of this: neither method may produce the right type of leader. In an election, a person's popularity rather than fitness for the task may influence the electors; and there may be the need for a corrective in the form of a committee of scrutiny. On the other hand, the method of patronage may involve a restriction on the range of candidates so that only 'safe' people are considered: William Temple himself doubted whether he would be selected as archbishop because of his outspokenness on public issues.

The question of the method of appointment thus cannot be considered in isolation from the question of the type of leader needed for the office; neither can it be considered apart from its interdependence with a whole range of personnel policies of which the actual appointment is the final stage.

In the Church of England, there is in fact a long process of selection and grooming for office prior to the actual appointment: it begins at school and continues through university, theological college, and career in the ministry (Morgan, 1963; Coxon, 1965). Hence a person who has been to the appropriate institutions and followed the recognized career pattern is likely to become a candidate for episcopal office; by contrast, a person who has not attended the appropriate institutions is likely to be excluded at the very start, not only from candidature, but from the earlier processes of selection and grooming.

The mere changing from royal patronage to election at the culmination of this process is unlikely to effect very much. The potential candidates for such an election would consist of those who had been prepared for office (who would have been chosen under the other method) and those who had had little opportunity for being prepared for high office (in which case they would be less likely to be elected; or, if elected, less likely to be worthy occupants of the office).

This does not mean that nothing should be done; rather, if the desire to be democratic (and the participation implicit in that approach is also essential in the systemic theory) is to be given effect, then much more needs to be done than changing the method of appointment: the whole process of training, selection, and preparation would need to be made more overt, and accessible to a wider range of potential candidates.

Nor can the mere change in the actual method of appointment necessarily be justified on the ground of adaptation to the environment. The method of election has developed most strongly in churches that have depended on participation by their members and that have been influenced by the democratic features of the society in which they exist. Thus, in many North American churches, for instance, election is the norm; but the imposition of a new method on a church like the Church of England (in which the traditional element is so strong) is not necessarily desirable. This church may not be immediately capable of the required level of sophistication; but there may be other ways in which the participative element could be introduced without making a radical alteration. The move to invite the opinion of a diocese on its needs may be a more appropriate way in that it reaches to more relevant issues than does an election on the ground of popularity.

The matter cannot, however, be considered as though the boundary of the Church of England were the limit of reference: the proposed union with the Methodists adds a new dimension to the decision, and if that challenge is rightly interpreted to the whole Church of England, there may well be some stimulus towards the resolution of the problem of the method of selection. An acceptable solution might be one that avoids the dichotomy in the current debate but takes into account the contributions of the respective practices in the two churches. A closely related issue which will also have to be resolved is tenure of office: whether it be for life or until voluntary retirement as in the Church of England, or whether it be for a short term as is common in the Methodist Church.

SECURITY OF TENURE

This question of security of tenure – another aspect of personnel policy – may be considered by reference to another topical document in the Church of England, namely, the Paul report (1964).

As its full title indicated, the report dealt with the deployment and payment of the clergy. The method of appointment on the parochial level which has prevailed for centuries in England has produced a pattern of deployment related to the existence of 'livings'; these benefices in turn were originally related to the village communities of feudal times. In the report, the essence of the analysis, which was supported by sociological evidence, was that the distribution of the clergy was seriously out of touch with the needs of a highly industrialized and urbanized Britain.

In order to effect a more adequate deployment, it was recommended that certain machinery be set up. There would be regional boards which would be responsible for the movement of clergy. However, it was recognized that the work of the boards would probably be frustrated by the unwillingness of clergy to move at the boards' direction or suggestion; the clergy could refuse to move on the basis of the existence of the parson's freehold, which gave them security of tenure. Once inducted to their incumbencies, they could remain there virtually for life, or at least until they were unable to fulfil some minimal legal requirements of their office; only in extreme circumstances could the clergy be deprived of their livings.

The report therefore proposed that the terms of tenure should be changed: the freehold should be transformed into a leasehold; security of tenure would be replaced by comparative insecurity; in the long run, then, clergy could not indefinitely postpone their acceptance of the recommendations of the regional boards.

In theoretical terms, the objective of adapting the deployment of the clergy to a changed environment was consonant with the systemic theory; but the method proposed was conceived in the mechanistic terms of the classical theory.

What are the alternative approaches to the question of security of tenure?

In the charismatic view, there is a premium on insecurity: there is a disregard for worldly things; the future is left in the hands of a divine power who will restore the fortunes of the elect in the age to come. The lack of security in the present age has its compensation in the security in the next. Typical of this attitude was the way William Temple (C1, p. 79) gave up a secure living to become the leader of the Life and Liberty Movement.

Lack of certainty about continuance in office is associated with the democratic approach, but there are usually some provisions to alleviate the insecurity. In some churches the leading officers are elected for a term of office – should they lose their position at a later election, they may be able to resume their former posts or move to some other office; in other churches leaders may be elected, but their appointments are for life or until retirement. There are usually safeguards to protect an elected leader from the mere whims of an electorate; there is also, while a person is in office, the satisfaction of serving, and of enjoying the confidence of, those who have placed him in that position.

The proposal put forward in the Paul report corresponded to neither of these forms of tenure: it was mainly in negative terms of taking away security and not putting anything in its place. It involved placing a limitation on the enjoyment of the freehold; beyond that limit, there would be insecurity.

Apparently it was not realized that there could be forms of freehold other than that which was attached to particular physical objects – a church, a vicarage, sometimes glebe lands, and the income pertaining to the particular benefice. Such a conception of freehold is typical of the traditional theory.

An alternative form of freehold, appropriate to the classical theory, is that attached to a specific office, an office within the pyramidal structure of the organization. Once a person is appointed to an office, he has the permanent right of occupancy and the income attaching thereto. He may seek higher office, but should he move up the hierarchy, he likewise has security within the new office. This conception avoids the particularism of the other form of freehold: no longer is it tied to a precise geographical place. But it can be just as rigid and incapable of change because of the clinging to a specific job when such a position may no longer be required in a changed organization.

A third form of freehold is that attaching to a profession, assuming that the ministry of the church will continue at least for some time on a full-time basis. Such a freehold would mean that the clergy would be fully provided for: they would have security of income and other benefits. Such emoluments would not be attached to physical objects or hierarchical positions but would be theirs by virtue of their ordination. The clergy would be free from the necessity to cling to particular places or jobs and so enabled to respond to whatever opportunities and challenges were presented in the world of complexity and change.

At the basis of this proposal is the recognition that the present form of freehold is in fact an umbrella for a wide range of specific areas of personnel policy. In its idealist form, it confers the right to preach the gospel without fear or favour; in reality, it is an amalgam of personnel measures.

The freehold is virtually a form of professional protection in that it is the means whereby a clergyman is shielded from indiscriminate action on the part of congregations or bishops or the proposed regional patronage boards. It is the source of his income and current housing. It covers his professional expenses or is assumed to do so. It is a form of provision for removal and settling-in expenses in that a new incumbent inherits the balance of the sequestration fund into which the income of the church has been paid during the interregnum. It is also a form of retirement benefit in that the clergyman has an income and a house virtually until his death. The freehold status is a career incentive: by contrast with an incumbent, an assistant curate is inferior in both income and status, so that there is an inducement to desire an incumbency without any necessary regard to other issues such as the needs of the church or of the man, which may be more important. Incumbencies are also graded: some are regarded as more desirable than others; some provide a greater income. Thus the existing freehold has within it what is in reality a whole system of career patterns and incentives.

If the freehold attaching to a particular place is to be transformed into a freehold attaching to the clerical profession, then action needs to be taken on all the above facets of personnel management. For instance, in place of the sequestration fund as the source of removal expenses, provision might be made from central diocesan or national sources. Action in this and the other areas is necessary so that a clergyman is not denied the benefits that he has enjoyed under the former kind of freehold. Where adequate alternative provision is made, he cannot plead deprivation in the face of any move that he may be called on to make in adapting to the new needs of the situation.

If he sees that he is to be properly provided for, he may be the more likely to respond; and there may then be less need to speak of compulsory transfers. A new incentive to respond could come from his realization of the needs and challenges of the church in a changing world; and it would be an important function of the leaders of the church to interpret the situation to the people whose co-operation is needed in attaining a new pattern of deployment.

PROMOTION, REMUNERATION, RETIREMENT BENEFITS

Other personnel issues are capable of treatment in the same way. On the issue of promotion, Paul (1964), working on the lines of the classical theory, proposed a career pattern that would offer clergy more opportunity at an intermediate level between the wide plateau occupied by ordinary parish clergy and the apex of the pyramid representing episcopal office: he suggested major parishes as another rank in the hierarchy. There are also clear consequences in terms of promotion arising from the systemic theory. The normal pattern of progression from deacon to priest to bishop is set aside; instead, there are three distinct career structures corresponding to the three functions envisaged in the theory. A person who enters the maintaining function can find the fulfilment of his career within that chosen area through taking more senior positions. From a small parish he could move to a larger, and so on to groups of parishes or to a diocesan position; and to the latter position the title of archdeacon properly belongs. Likewise, a minister could spend his whole life in the performance of the ministering function: he could be upgraded by moving to more important and larger parishes or to more specialized work; and there could be officers in a diocese – like many assistant bishops at present – whose responsibility was for the fulfilling of the ministering function on that level. This could be a worthwhile career. Others may choose or be selected for the performance of the monitoring function; and for these men there could be a satisfying progression from posts of lesser to posts of greater responsibility, eventually leading to episcopal or primatial office.

Remuneration is another major component of personnel management. On this issue, mention has been made of Scherer's comparison (1965a) between the patrimonial-patronage method and that appropriate to the bureaucratic or classical theory. The systemic approach follows the latter in its emphasis on the single salary source; but it is more universal in its operation in that the classical method is usually tied to a particular office whereas the systemic is related to the profession, as noted in the comments on the Paul report. A man is ordained as a priest in the church of God; but in many cases his income is derived by virtue of his being the minister of a particular parish. A more universal method is needed so that the personnel policy reflects the character of the office; more appropriate would be a policy on the diocesan or national level so that a man could serve where needed without being subjected to the anomalies of several paying authorities.

Superannuation and retirement benefits also require attention. A development in these fields in the light of the systemic theory was the way in which the Anglican Church of Canada, for instance, devised a pension formula that took into account the changes, especially the rises, in the cost of living. Likewise, in an Australian diocese, the retirement annuity is related not to a fixed amount but to the average stipend over the five years prior to relinquishing office.

HOUSING

There is great variation in the housing policies for ministers according to the several theories.

The traditional policy is usually expressed in the form of a residence adjacent to the church; in some cases it may even be physically joined to it (thus eliminating the possibility of any alternative use). The closeness of the residence to the church reflects the fusion of the minister's private and public spheres of life; there is little privacy for the minister, or for his family, who are implicated in much of what goes on in the church. The home cannot be a private refuge: it has to be open to the demands of callers of all kinds; and it is not uncommon for the vicarage to be invaded by parishioners. The consequences of this policy on marital harmony and on the character of ministers' children have yet to be estimated. The difficulty of the situation in England is increased by the fact that many vicarages were built in the days of a society in which maids, servants, and valets were common – many vicarages are much too large to be managed by a wife who does not have such household assistance. The costs of maintenance and heating can be prohibitive as well (A4, p. 78).

Housing is not a concern for a charismatic type of leader: it would be a distraction from his calling to be involved in such worldly matters. How many wives and children suffer from such an other-worldly attitude! The itinerant preacher has no need to think of such things;

he needs only temporary accommodation at each place and he has no thought about a permanent residence.

Housing policies can also be shaped in terms of the classical theory. In the Church of England the specifications for a vicarage require a certain number of rooms of a certain size, seemingly on the assumption that all clergymen have a family of a standard size. Such a building can be a source of considerable embarrassment to a single man or a young couple without children: furnishing, upkeep, and heating would be on a larger scale than they would desire or could afford. The cost of construction would be a financial embarrassment to the local church; and the resulting building could well be an anomaly in, say, a working-class area where it separated the vicar from the general standards of his people. Furthermore, it would be of such permanence that it could become redundant in a future redevelopment of housing. In some Methodist circuits the policy has been to provide not only the house but all its fittings, furnishings, curtains, even the linen; there would be a saving in removal costs, but such a policy presupposes not only standardized families but also standardized tastes as to décor.

Exponents of the human relations theory would protest against this regimentation, and this is a stepping-stone towards the systemic policy about clergy housing, which allows a high degree of flexibility on such items as family size and preferences about the style of house and the kind of decoration. Moreover, it ensures the privacy of the minister and his family, such as other families enjoy.

The provision of a house, particularly close to the church, is typical of the traditional policy of remuneration – income is given in kind, and this is one of a number of income sources. The alternative is to pay the full stipend in cash, including the equivalent of the house in the form of a living allowance. The advantages of each of these policies were indicated in an article by C. Russell Stout entitled 'Manse or Living Allowance' (1965):

> This question is becoming more and more prominent in churches of all sizes. There are advantages to both sides of the issue. Let us look first to the policy of church-owned property.
>
> One of the foremost factors is that of the church's image to the community. A large auspicious, well-kept and cared-for manse or parsonage is something to be proud of by the congregation and something to be admired by members of other churches – somewhat like a 'keeping up with the Jones' situation. In the same vein, many

clergymen, especially those with college age children, and in view of the advancing cost of living, could not afford the type of dwelling expected of their position.

In many cases the pastor and his family are expected to host both church and social events in their home. There is a possibility of some false feeling of restraint by the church members with other than church-owned property.

An item that all property-owners face is that of upkeep. Lawns, gardens, outside paint and roofs as well as plumbing, mechanical and redecoration work must constantly be reckoned with. With a manse provided, none of these problems need be a burden on the busy pastor or his family.

Another problem in changing to the allowance policy might be the disposition of the present church-owned property.

Examing the allowance route, we find the arguments seem to favor this method. Foremost on this side is the feeling of ownership, and family pride that is present when a family 'buys a home'. Even if a pastor stays but a few years, the family builds up some equity in their property.

From the church board's viewpoint, a great advantage lies in the fact that an allowance is a constant amount throughout, at least, the budget year. No extra amount need be set aside for emergency repairs or unexpected expenses. No embarrassing inspection visits need be made to see if the property is being properly maintained. No misunderstanding results as to whether a room or rooms need re-decoration. This can be left to the family as to their desires and needs.

The misfortune of moving a newly married couple into an over-sized, multi-roomed manse is deplorable. This is even worse than moving a family with 4 or 5 children into an undersized house. How much more practical it is for a family to choose the size, location and type of home that is suited to their needs.

The method of deciding the amount of the 'living expenses' allowance naturally will vary with the size and needs of the church. A simple method of coming to this amount is to have a committee determine the costs to the church of owning and maintaining the present manse or parsonage. All costs should be considered: utilities, yard upkeep and the original investment in the property. Even if the home has been a gift, a real estate agent can determine a fair cost. In some cases the family occupying a home like it so well they would welcome a chance to buy it from the church, at a fair price. This, too, can be done with advantage.

In some or even many cases, the problem of a down payment can be a stumbling block for a clergyman. Loan agencies and banks are historically liberal in their terms to the clergy, especially with good co-signers from the church membership. Some arrangement can surely be made to finance this step.

Pastors and Boards alike should investigate and study the advantages that can be obtained by both parties in an allowance type of arrangement. Tax consultants can point out perfectly legitimate tax savings to the pastor under this method and as more and more states are removing the church-owned properties from the tax rolls, the church itself may find a tax advantage here. Consider it well, Boards, as you may put new joy in your pastor's life at no extra cost to the church.

Regardless of the policy chosen, the official board should ask its Property Committee to evaluate the present needs of their church.

A notable illustration of the latter policy is that of a church which bought the house that the new minister chose; when the house was sold on his departure some years later, the church simply recouped its outlay and gave the appreciation in its value to the minister.

The adoption of this policy assumes the existence of freehold housing; but such a condition does not always apply in England: on some housing estates, dwellings are available only on lease, and in many cases the buildings are of a standard size and not necessarily suitable as clergy residences. In one such situation the following recommendations were made (Rudge, 1966b, p. 31):

Perhaps the most satisfactory thing to do is to buy houses suited to the needs and desires of the various clergymen, as has been done with the house in Whinmoor Gardens. But the difficulty is that there are few houses that can be bought in Seacroft unless there be a major change in Corporation policy. Houses may be rented, but these are not necessarily suitable for clergy residences – there is no room other than the lounge that is accessible without interfering with the rest of the house and which can be used as a study-consulting room.

Hence the solution seems to be to build suitable houses on the freehold land that is available in the several places, especially at St James's. Advantage could be taken of the system-built houses which are at present being erected on the estates; these would probably cost much less than conventional buildings. They could probably be designed to meet the needs of clergy residences. This does not mean that they would all be of the same size; there should be variety ranging from bachelor flats to four-bedroom houses with provision for studies. This would mean that there would be suitable sized homes for the clergy whether they were single or married and whether they had small or large families. Such houses should also be sited so that they could be let to others should they not be required for church purposes.

The adoption of a housing-allowance policy necessitates certain other steps, such as the provision of clergy offices at the church, the introduction of a telephone system similar to that of group practices of doctors, and the engagement of a secretary-telephonist to take over the duties that the wife performed in the traditional arrangement.

CONCLUSION

The foregoing treatment does not exhaust either the list of topics or the content of the respective theories, but it indicates some of the notable divergences that there are between the several personnel policies and perhaps prepares the way for a fuller discussion.

In conclusion, it is worth noting some of the important guidelines for the development of personnel policies in keeping with the systemic theory. Every aspect of personnel management must be overtly recognized and consciously provided for; but each aspect can be considered only in relation to adjacent areas of concern. The objectives are to strengthen the commitment of clergy to the total purpose of the church, to prepare them for their responsibilities, and to allow them maximum mobility and security in the fulfilling of their duties. The appropriate provision is an essential element in the adoption of the systemic theory as the most adequate guide in the whole area of life included in the study of ecclesiastical administration.

References

ABRECHT, PAUL (1961). *The Churches and Rapid Social Change.* Garden City, N.Y.: Doubleday.

ADAIR, JOHN (1962). A Staff College for the Church of England. *Theology*, **65** (503), May.

— (1968). *Training for Leadership.* London: Macdonald.

ADAMS, ARTHUR MERRIHEW (1964). *Pastoral Administration.* Philadelphia, Pa.: The Westminster Press.

ANGLICAN CHURCH OF CANADA (1965). *Journal of Proceedings of General Synod.*

BARNARD, CHESTER I. (1938). *The Functions of the Executive.* Cambridge, Mass.: Harvard University Press.

BELL, G. K. A. (1935). *Randall Davidson: Archbishop of Canterbury.* 2 vols. London: Oxford University Press.

BENNIS, WARREN G. (1959). Leadership Theory and Administrative Behavior: The Problem of Authority. *Administrative Science Quarterly*, **4** (3), December.

BLACKWOOD, ANDREW WATTERSON (1949). *Pastoral Leadership.* New York: Abingdon-Cokesbury Press.

BLIZZARD, SAMUEL W. (1956). *The Urban Parish Minister and his Training Needs.* A confidential mimeographed report on a project initiated by the Russell Sage Foundation.

BOOZ, ALLEN & HAMILTON (1963). *Report on Governing Structure of the National Council of the Churches of Christ in the United States of America.* Private consultancy report to the Special Committee on Structure and Function of the National Council of Churches.

BURNS, TOM & STALKER, G. M. (1961). *The Management of Innovation.* London: Tavistock Publications.

Church Administration. Monthly. The Sunday School Board, Southern Baptist Convention, 127 Ninth Avenue North, Nashville 3, Tennessee.

Church Management. Monthly. Church Management, Inc., 2491 Lee Boulevard, Cleveland Heights 18, Ohio.

CHURCH OF ENGLAND BOARD OF EDUCATION (1965). *Consultation on Small Group Work for Staffs of Teacher Training Colleges.* London: Church of England Board of Education.

COX, HARVEY (1965). *The Secular City*. New York: Macmillan; London: SCM Press.

COXON, ANTHONY P. M. (1965). *A Sociological Study of the Social Recruitment, Selection, and Professional Socialization of Anglican Ordinands*. Unpublished Ph.D. thesis, University of Leeds.

CROSS, F. L. (ed.) (1957). *The Oxford Dictionary of the Christian Church* London: Oxford University Press.

Crown Appointments and the Church (C.A. 1534) (1964). Westminster: Church Information Office.

DADY, ROBERT L. (1961). *The Church as an Institution, with special reference for Unity*. Unpublished S.T.M. thesis, School of Theology, Boston University.

DENN, DON FRANK (1938). *Parish Administration*. New York: Morehouse Gorham.

DITZEN, LOWELL RUSSELL (1962). *Handbook of Church Administration*. New York: Macmillan.

DOBBINS, GAINES S. (1960). *The Ministering Church*. Nashville, Tenn.: Boardman Press.

DONNISON, D. V.; CHAPMAN, VALERIE; MEACHER, MICHAEL; SEARS, ANGELA & URWIN, KENNETH (1965). *Social Policy and Administration*. London: Allen & Unwin.

DUCOS, MARCEL, O.P. (1963). *Pour un Apostolat Organisé*. Paris: Fleurus.

EHRENSTROM, NILS & MUELDER, WALTER G. (eds.) (1963). *Institutionalism and Church Unity*. New York: Association Press; London: SCM Press.

ETZIONI, AMITAI (1961). *A Comparative Analysis of Complex Organizations*. New York: The Free Press of Glencoe.

Faith and Order Findings (1963). The Report of the Study Commission on Institutionalism. Faith and Order Paper No. 37. London: SCM Press.

FERRIS, PAUL (1962). *The Church of England*. London: Gollancz; New York: Macmillan, 1963.

FICHTER, JOSEPH H. (1961). *Religion as an Occupation*. South Bend, Indiana: University of Notre Dame Press.

FIRST PRESBYTERIAN CHURCH (1963). *A Handbook to Help Acquaint You with First Presbyterian Church, Fort Wayne, Indiana*.

FORDER, CHARLES R. (1947). *The Parish Priest at Work*. Second edition 1959. London: SPCK.

FRANCIS, E. K. (1950). Toward a Typology of Religious Orders. *American Journal of Sociology*, 55 (5), March.

GOULDNER, ALVIN W. (1954). *Patterns of Industrial Bureaucracy.* Glencoe, Ill.: The Free Press; London: Routledge & Kegan Paul, 1955.

HARRISON, PAUL M. (1959). *Authority and Power in the Free Church Tradition: A Social Case Study of the American Baptist Convention.* Princeton, N.J.: Princeton University Press; London: Oxford University Press, 1960.

—— (1960). Weber's Categories of Authority and Voluntary Associations. *American Sociological Review*, **25** (2), April.

—— (1965). Guidelines for Research on Inter-Protestant Relations. *Information Service*, **44** (2), 16 January. New York: National Council of Churches.

IREMONGER, F. A. (1948). *William Temple: Archbishop of Canterbury.* Abridged edition, 1963. London: Oxford University Press.

KIRK, KENNETH E. (1955). *Beauty and Bands.* London: Hodder & Stoughton; New York: The Seabury Press.

LEACH, WILLIAM H. (1958). *Handbook of Church Management.* Englewood Cliffs, N.J.: Prentice-Hall; London: Bailey & Swinfen.

LIKERT, RENSIS (1961). *New Patterns of Management.* New York: McGraw-Hill.

LLOYD, ROGER (1946–50). *The Church of England in the Twentieth Century.* 2 vols. London: Longmans, Green. Revised edition entitled *The Church of England 1900–1965.* London: SCM Press, 1966. (Extract quoted on p. 86 of this volume is not included in the revised edition.)

LOCKHART, J. G. (1949). *Cosmo Gordon Lang.* London: Hodder & Stoughton; New York: Macmillan.

MCGREGOR, DOUGLAS (1960). *The Human Side of Enterprise.* New York: McGraw-Hill.

MALDEN, R. H. (1935). *A Short History of the Diocese of Ripon 1836–1936* (n.p.).

MARTIN, D. A. (1962). The Denomination. *British Journal of Sociology*, **13** (1), March.

MAYO, ELTON (1933). *The Human Problems of an Industrial Civilization.* New York: Macmillan; London: Routledge & Kegan Paul.

MENGES, ROBERT J. & DITTES, JAMES E. (1965). *Psychological Studies of Clergymen.* Camden, N.J.: Nelson.

MINEAR, PAUL S. (1960). *Images of the Church in the New Testament.* Philadelphia, Pa.: The Westminster Press; London: Lutterworth Press, 1961.

MOBERG, DAVID O. (1962). *The Church as a Social Institution: The Sociology of American Religion.* Englewood Cliffs, N.J.: Prentice-Hall.

MOBERLY, R. C. (1899). *Ministerial Priesthood.* Second edition. London: Murray.

MOONEY, J. D. & REILEY, A. C. (1931). *Onward Industry!* New York: Harper. Republished 1939 as *The Principles of Organization.* Revised edition, MOONEY, J. D., New York: Harper, 1947.

MORGAN, D. H. J. (1963). *The Social and Educational Background of English Diocesan Bishops in the Church of England 1860–1960.* Unpublished M.A. thesis, University of Hull.

NATIONAL COUNCIL OF CHURCHES (n.d.). Introducing Organizational Analysis. New York.

NEAL, SR. MARIE AUGUSTA, S.N.D. (1965). *Values and Interests in Social Change.* Englewood Cliffs, N.J.: Prentice-Hall.

New Christian. Fortnightly. Prism Publications, Blue Star House, Highgate Hill, London, N 19.

NEWMAN, JEREMIAH (1965). *Change and the Catholic Church.* Baltimore, Md., and Dublin: Helicon.

NIEBUHR, H. RICHARD (1951). *Christ and Culture.* New York: Harper.

—— (1956). *The Purpose of the Church and its Ministry.* New York: Harper.

Parish and People. Quarterly. Prism Publications, Blue Star House, Highgate Hill, London, N 19.

PAUL, LESLIE (1964). *The Deployment and Payment of the Clergy.* Westminster: Church Information Office.

PAUL, RAJAIAH D. (1958). *The First Decade: An Account of the Church of South India.* Madras: The Christian Literature Society.

PRICE, DEREK (1963). *Unity in Itself: The Stevenage Experiment in Group Ministry.* London: SPCK.

PRICE WATERHOUSE & CO. (1964). *The Anglican Church of Canada in the Diocese of Rupert's Land: A Plan for Operating the Diocese More Effectively.* Winnipeg. Unpublished consultancy report.

Prism. Discontinued. Prism Publications, Blue Star House, Highgate Hill, London, N 19.

REDDIN, W. J. (1964). The Tri-Dimensional Grid. *Training Directors Journal,* July.

RIDLEY Report (1956). *Report of the Committee on Central Funds (C.A. 1181).* Westminster: The Church Information Board.

ROBINSON, J. A. T. (1960). The Priesthood and the Church. In *Essays on Being the Church in the World.* London: SCM Press; Philadelphia, Pa.: The Westminster Press, 1962.

—— (1961). A New Model of Episcopacy. In Bishop of Llandaff (ed.), *Bishops.* London: The Faith Press.

—— (1965). *The New Reformation?* London: SCM Press; Philadelphia, Pa.: The Westminster Press.

RUDGE, P. F. (1964). *A New Approach to the Study of Ecclesiastical Administration.* Unpublished diploma thesis, St Augustine's College, Canterbury.

—— (1966a). *The Study of Ecclesiastical Administration using the Methods and Insights of Public Administration.* Unpublished Ph.D. thesis, University of Leeds.

—— (1966b). *The Parish of Seacroft: A New Creation.* Privately circulated consultancy report.

SCHERER, ROSS P. (1964). Income and Business Costs of the Protestant Clergy in 1963 – a Preliminary Report of a National Council of Churches' Survey of Clergy Support. *Information Service,* **43** (19), 5 December. New York: National Council of Churches.

—— (1965a). The Ministry and its Sources of Income. *Seminary Quarterly,* **6** (11), Winter. Minneapolis, Minn.: Ministers Life and Casualty Union.

—— (1965b). The White Protestant Denominations: Some Central Tendencies and Variations in their Clergy. Paper presented at meeting of the American Sociological Association, Chicago.

SIMON, HERBERT A. (1945). *Administrative Behavior.* Second edition, 1957. New York: Macmillan.

SIMON, HERBERT A.; SMITHBURG, DONALD W. & THOMPSON, VICTOR A. (1950). *Public Administration.* New York: Knopf.

SIMPSON, JOHN H. (1965). *A Study of the Role of the Protestant Parish Minister with special reference to Organization Theory.* Unpublished Master of Theology thesis, Princeton Theological Seminary, Princeton, N.J.

SMYTH, CHARLES (1959). *Cyril Forster Garbett: Archbishop of York.* London: Hodder & Stoughton.

SPENCER, A. E. C. W. (1963). The Span of Control, Scalar Development and the Structure of the Church's Administration. Paper read to the Canon Law Society, London.

—— (1966). The Catholic Church in England. In J. D. Halloran & Joan Brothers (eds.), *Uses of Sociology.* London: Sheed & Ward.

STOUT, C. RUSSELL (1965). Manse or Living Allowance. *Church Management,* December.

THOMPSON, RICHARD H. T. (1957). *Training for the Ministry: An Exploratory Study.* Christchurch, N.Z.: Presbyterian Bookroom.

TÖNNIES, FERDINAND (1955). *Community and Association: Gemeinschaft und Gesellschaft.* Trans. & suppl. Charles P. Loomis. London: Routledge & Kegan Paul.

URWICK, L. (1944). *The Elements of Administration.* New York: Harper. Second edition, London: Pitman, 1947.

VAN VLECK, JOSEPH, JR. (1937). *Our Changing Churches: A Study of Leadership.* New York: Association Press.

WEBER, MAX (1947). *The Theory of Social and Economic Organization.* Trans. A. M. Henderson & Talcott Parsons; ed. Talcott Parsons. Glencoe, Ill.: The Free Press; Edinburgh: Hodge. Second edition, Glencoe, Ill.: The Free Press, 1957.

WELCH, ADAM C. (1936). *Prophet and Priest in Old Israel.* London: SCM Press.

WORSLEY, PETER (1957). *The Trumpet Shall Sound: A Study of 'Cargo' Cults in Melanesia.* London: MacGibbon & Kee.

FURTHER READING ON THE SYSTEMIC THEORY

In view of the comparative unfamiliarity of the systemic theory, further literature is suggested below. On the general concept of a system:

TIMASHEFF, NICHOLAS S. (1957). *Sociological Theory: Its Nature and Growth.* Revised edition. New York: Random House.

Other works in the managerial and organizational field are:

BEER, STAFFORD (1959). *Cybernetics and Management.* London: English Universities Press; New York: Wiley, 1960.

BENNIS, WARREN G. (1965). Beyond Bureaucracy. *Trans-action,* 2 (5), July-August.

FOLLETT, MARY PARKER (1949). *Dynamic Administration: The Collected Papers of Mary Parker Follett.* Ed. Henry C. Metcalf & L. Urwick. New York: Harper; London: Management Publications.

HARTUNG, L. P. & MORGAN, J. E. (1961). *PERT/PEP . . . A Dynamic Project Control Method.* Owego, N.Y.: FSD Space Guidance Center.

HEYEL, CARL (ed.) (1964). s.v. Systems and Procedures. *The Encyclopedia of Management.* New York: Reinhold; London: Chapman & Hall.

JOHNSON, RICHARD A.; KAST, FREMONT E. & ROSENZWEIG, JAMES E. (1963). *The Theory and Management of Systems.* New York: McGraw-Hill.

MILLER, E. J. & RICE, A. K. (1967). *Systems of Organization.* London: Tavistock Publications.

RICE, A. K. (1963). *The Enterprise and its Environment.* London: Tavistock Publications.

TILLES, SEYMOUR (1963). The Manager's Job: A Systems Approach. *Harvard Business Review,* 41 (1), January.

TRIST, E. L.; HIGGIN, G. W.; MURRAY, H. & POLLOCK, A. B. (1963). *Organizational Choice.* London: Tavistock Publications.

WOLF, WILLIAM B. (1956). Organizational Constructs: An Approach to Understanding Organizations. Paper presented to the Research Society of the College of Business Administration, University of Washington, Seattle, Wash.

On the concept of a system in political science, see:

ALMOND, GABRIEL A. & COLEMAN, JAMES S. (eds.) (1960). *The Politics of Developing Areas.* Princeton, N.J.: Princeton University Press; London: Oxford University Press.

BEER, SAMUEL H. (1962). The Analysis of Political Systems. In Samuel H. Beer & Adam B. Ulam (eds.), *Patterns of Government: The Major Political Systems of Europe.* Second edition, revised and enlarged. New York: Random House.

GROSS, BERTRAM M. (1966). *The State of the Nation.* London: Tavistock Publications.

WOLIN, SHELDON S. (1960). *Politics and Vision.* Boston, Mass.: Little, Brown; London: Allen & Unwin, 1961.

Author Index

Subject Index